RETHINKING THE HUMAN

A volume in the Center for the Study of World Religions' series: Studies in World Religions

Other volumes recently published by the Center for the Study of World Religions and available through Harvard University Press:

- *Ecology and the Environment: Perspectives from the Humanities,* Donald K. Swearer, ed. Religions of the World and Ecology Series

- *Religion and Nationalism in Iraq: A Comparative Perspective,* David Little and Donald K. Swearer, eds. Studies in World Religions Series

RETHINKING THE HUMAN

Edited by J. Michelle Molina and Donald K. Swearer

with Susan Lloyd McGarry

Center for the Study of World Religions
Harvard Divinity School
Cambridge, Massachusetts
Distributed by Harvard University Press
2010

Cover Art and Design: Kristie Welsh

Library of Congress Cataloging-in-Publication Data

Rethinking the human / edited by J. Michelle Molina and Donald K.
Swearer with Susan Lloyd McGarry.
    p. cm. -- (Studies in world religions)
  Includes bibliographical references and index.
  ISBN 978-0-945454-44-1 (pbk. : alk. paper) 1. Humanity. 2. Ethics. I.
Molina, J. Michelle. II. Swearer, Donald K., 1934- III. McGarry, Susan
Lloyd. IV. Title. V. Series.

BJ1533.H9R48 2010
170--dc22

                                                    2010000982

Contents

Preface

Donald K. Swearer

Since 1958 the Center for the Study of World Religions (CSWR) at Harvard Divinity School (HDS) has conceived research and dialogue in the field of world religions in broad, interdisciplinary terms. For the past five years, the Center has sponsored symposia, films, lectures, and other programs focused on a particular theme for the year. For the academic year 2007–08 and in this volume, the Center concentrated on "Rethinking the Human." At a time when existing views of the human condition are being challenged by developments in the biological sciences, cultural studies, and global ethical norms, the CSWR explored the very notion of what it means to be human from interdisciplinary, cross-cultural, and multireligious perspectives. In broad overarching terms, "Rethinking the Human" asked whether meaningful general claims can be made in regard to the human, human nature, human values, human rights, human capabilities and the like, or whether all meaningful claims about the human and hyphenated human qualities and activities are necessarily limited, contextual, and contingent. Or, as several papers in this volume suggest, the interpretative lens of contextual versus universal may need to be contested as part of rethinking the human. The theme's announcement posed the question this way: "In our globalized world, seemingly different conceptions of human nature and human values raise critical questions as to whether universal and partisan claims, interests, and perspectives can be reconciled, whether interreligious and intercultural conversations can have a positive effect on building human community, and whether a pluralistic ethos can effectively transcend the uncompromising notions now current as to what is true, good, necessary, just, and real."

The presenters' disciplines and their topics embodied the

multireligious, interdisciplinary goals of this series, as can be seen from the list of speakers:

- Abdullahi Ahmed An-Na'im, the Charles Chandler Professor of Law, Emory University, "Who Is the 'Human' in 'Human Rights'?"
- Laurie Zoloth, Director of the Center for Bioethics, Science and Society and Professor of Medical Humanities, Bioethics, and Religion, Northwestern University, "Bioscience and the Alteration of Human Limits";
- Christine Korsgaard, Arthur Kingsley Porter Professor of Philosophy and Director of Graduate Studies in Philosophy, "Humanity, Ethics, and Our Animal Nature"
- Tu Weiming, then Harvard-Yenching Professor of Chinese History and Philosophy and Confucian Studies, and Director of the Harvard-Yenching Institute, "Is There an Innate Sense of Morality?"
- Sudhir Kakar, psychoanalyst and author, Goa, India, "Imagination and What It Means To Be Human."

We chose respondents to the lecturers who could engage the position developed by the speakers from different religious, cultural, and disciplinary perspectives. How might a human rights lawyer or a Buddhist philosopher respond to An-Na'im's question of whether human rights can be defined as universal in the light of the realities of profound cultural and religious differences? A medical ethicist or a scholar of Japanese Buddhism to Zoloth's analysis of biotechnology enhancements and alterations to human physical, intellectual and moral limits? Similarly we asked a scholar of Native American religion and a director of a center for animals and public policy in a medical school to respond to Korsgaard's Kantian argument that humans have duties to other animals and are committed to including animal welfare in any assessment we make of the goodness of the world. A developmental psychologist and a pioneer in the intersection of psychology and neuroscience each responded to Weiming's exposition of a Neo-Confucian view that although moral feelings such as compassion can be cultivated they are essentially innate. We asked a Western rationalist to respond to Kukar's talk on how "connective imagination" conjoining humankind to the universe should be central to emerging images of humanity. The dialectical engagement among speaker, respondents, and audience did not offer final answers to such questions, but it succeeded in illustrating the rich complexities of what it means to be human and challenged any singular, definitive answer to that question. We recorded these talks, responses, and the discussions following and have posted them on our website by speaker name (http://www.hds.harvard.edu/cswr/resources/lectures/index.html).

The May 2008 CSWR capstone conference that concluded the year's thematic programming encompassed a similarly wide spectrum of disciplines and topics—anthropology and medical anthropology; intellectual history and comparative religions; social ethics and English literature; India, China, and the West; historical, modern, and contemporary-present. The essays included in this volume were first presented at that conference and then further developed by the essayists.

In his lecture, "The Fractured World of Humanity," Michael Puett, a scholar of Chinese history, brings a civilizational, cross-cultural perspective to bear on the topic of rethinking the human. Using classical Chinese Confucian texts—*Mencius, Xunzi, Xing zi ming chu*—Puett challenges a conventional understanding of the classical Chinese worldview as being fundamentally harmonious. He argues, rather, that these texts assume a fractured universe. Consequently, the goal of being fully human is to work ceaselessly to transform the world even though it is recognized that these periods of transformation will be only temporary. How does this come about? Puett sees the Confucian ritual system as a strategy for developing the positive dispositions such as compassion that will heal the fractures among humans, nonhumans, and the cosmos.

If Puett brings a macrocosmic, civilizational perspective to the topic of rethinking the human, the lectures by Arthur Kleinman, Veena Das, Lila Abu-Lughod, and Charles Hallisey focus on the microcosmic—the individual in relational situations. Kleinman, a prominent medical anthropologist and psychiatrist, explores caregiving as the quotidian context in which we are most fully human—not a state of Mencian harmony or Buddhist ethical perfection—but a condition in which we fully embrace our dividedness between frustration and despair, compassion and solidarity that elicits a "fuller, more human presence than we ever realized we possessed." Kleinman makes the practical point that when viewed form the vantage point of caregiving, the topic of rethinking the human moves from the world of discourse to an engagement with the stubbornness of things: "The grounding of experience in the reality of caregiving shows us how practice leads the way to the moral."

Veena Das and Lila Abu-Lughod, both anthropologists with extensive experience in the field, address the question of what it means to be human from a communal, anthropological fieldwork perspective. Das shares Kleinman's quotidian, existential point of view, namely, that the "human" is to be understood in terms of the challenges and trials of living, as Das puts it, "when someone responds to events that put his or her entire life into question." As with Kleinman's caregiver, it is Das' slum-dwelling Delhi protagonist, Billu's openness to the "other"—both human and nonhuman—mother, wife, son, ghost, goddess—that comes to define his humanity in terms of its limitations and possibilities. Abu-Lughod turns our attention from a Delhi slum to a family in Egypt, who befriended her when she first began her fieldwork as a young graduate student. Of all the papers in this volume, Abu-Lughod critiques most fully the problematic of "rethinking the human" from the perspective of the polarity of the particular and contextual versus the general and universal. She proposes a different approach ("another dialect"), one she characterized in her monograph, *Writing Women's Worlds,* as a "tactical humanism" that avoids the pitfalls of universals as in "universal human rights," whether liberal secular or liberal feminist, or mere cultural particularity. She puts it this way, "My stories from Egypt about the Haj [the Bedouin-born paterfamilias of that Egyptian family] suggest that we do not actually need this mediating code [i.e., universal human rights] to speak to each other. When I reflect on my relationship with him and his family, I am tempted to turn to another metaphor of universality that is also embedded in the language of the human. What if we took more seriously as a model not the fantasy of 'universality' but the 'family of man.' " [Material in brackets my addition.]

Charles Hallisey, a scholar of Buddhism, also explores the topic of rethinking the human microscopically. In this case, the microscope is on his aging mother rather than an individual embedded in a particular social or kinship context. With allusions to Charles Péguy, Theodor Adorno, Yukio Mishima, Shinran, Buddhaghosa, and others, Hallisey makes the provocative proposal that to fail to consider the image of the human at ninety would be to distort other images of the human that we might investigate. Hallisey suggests that an existential understanding of what it means to be human calls for another kind of contextualization by age, not only by gender, social hierarchy, geography, and so on. Furthermore, in "eavesdropping" (looking "sideways") on his mother in her old age, Hallisey not only learns something about her, but about himself; indeed, something about what it means to be human.

Two papers not included here also helped to set the tone. They addressed what it means to be human in terms of the "barbarisms" of our times, but from very different perspectives. With allusions to Walter Benjamin, T.S. Eliot, Hannah Arendt, Jacques Derrida, and Ian McEwan, Homi Bhabha, Harvard's Anne F. Rothenberg Professor of the Humanities, explored the transmission of barbarism in cultural memory from the events of Nuremberg, the Holocaust, landscapes of *jihad,* and the war on terror, to more abstract notions of the intense suffering of quotidian endlessness, and war as metaphor for the messianic struggle for the soul. These references were juxtaposed with the dialectic of ambivalence in the midst of dissonance recalling Habermas, the tolerance to endure the contingency of enmeshed contradiction, and an ethic of endurance. John P. Reeder, Jr. Visiting Professor of Ethics, Harvard Divinity School and Professor Emeritus of Religion, Brown University, explored philosophical debates about noncombatant immunity in circumstances of extreme emergency that threaten to destroy the very existence of political communities. Is there a way out of the moral ambiguity of such decisions? In what way(s) do such "barbarisms" challenge the moral limits of how we understand the human, human rights, human values?

Dozens of scholars at Harvard and from other universities in this country and internationally were part of the planning and presentation of the CSWR 2007–2008 programming on "Rethinking the Human." Co-sponsors who supported and participated in the lectures and conference included the Harvard-Yenching Institute and the Humanities Center at Harvard. I am particularly grateful to Homi Bhabha, Director of the Humanities Center at Harvard; Tu Weiming, then Harvard-Yenching Professor of Chinese History and Philosophy and Confucian Studies, and Director of the Harvard-Yenching Institute; and Michael Jackson, Distinguished Visiting Professor of World Religions at Harvard Divinity School, who played a major role in conceptualizing and planning the theme's programs. I would also like to thank Joe Cook, CSWR staff assistant, and Ailya Vajid, an HDS student assistant, for their careful proofreading and help with reference-checking for this volume.

Donald K. Swearer
Director, Center for the Study of World Religions
Distinguished Visiting Professor of Buddhist Studies
Harvard Divinity School

Introduction: An Ambivalent Philosophy of the Concrete

J. Michelle Molina[1]

What does it mean to rethink the human? Mundane routines of daily life play a key role in these essays devoted to exploring this question. These scholars are at home in the world, their careers enmeshed in multiple life-worlds. They brought their experiences back to a Harvard conference room and to the page to meditate on how the particularity of those experiences can reshape Western universals. Asked to "rethink the human"—a daunting task—they self-consciously attempted to undertake the project so as to avoid donning the straightjacket of a new universalism. Particularly important is the way the life-cycles of loved ones figured into analyses about a human experience that is "universal," yet, experienced uniquely. Despite the variety of contexts under discussion, the participants responded that we know ourselves in and through the particularity of relationships. How can we know "the human" but for our compulsion to know and live alongside one another?

Life stories emerge from intersubjective relationships. As anthropologist Michael Jackson has written in *Minima Ethnographica*, the attempt toward knowing another is neither utopian nor cognitive. Drawing upon phenomenologist Maurice Merleau-Ponty, Jackson reminds us that intersubjectivity is actively conditioned by a repertoire of "reciprocal gestures, common metaphors, parallel images and shared intentions."[2] Both the day of the conference and in reading and editing these essays, I have thought about what it means to exist in the interstices between self and other, and also how this relates to the way we do our work in the academy—our common metaphors, gestures, intentions. What does it mean to examine the particularities of everyday life and then link them, as Charles Hallisey commented, gesturing toward the podium, walls, and seats of the Sperry Room, to "what we do in this room"? What is it that we do "in the world" and then what do we do with those "doings" in places like the Sperry Room? When academics tell these narratives in wood-paneled conference rooms, another level of meaning-making extends beyond the narrative itself. We could characterize these reports of findings-from-the-field as "performance." In the performative aspect of the intellectual endeavor, the authors' exquisite deliveries kept us (the audience) pinned to our seats as we leaned forward to hear more about these experiences, connected to another's narrative. "Gripping" is not a word often used to describe a day-long conference. Yet there was a remarkable urgency, an intangible dynamic between speakers and audience members who found something too close to home, a shared endeavor, perhaps the shared "universal" experience of living and dying. Given the resonance that the stories we told ourselves about ourselves had in the Sperry Room, this was clearly "deep play" in the sense of anthropologist Clifford Geertz.[3] The stakes were high. But why? What was so compelling?

I can only offer a sense of what held me to my own seat for the entire day. Part of it was a mood of nostalgia. A fabulous year as a visiting scholar and fellow in the Women's Studies in Religion Program was drawing to a close. Perhaps tenured faculty grow blasé about being in Cambridge, but I knew I had been spoiled by access to an amazing library system, the camaraderie of a fabulous group of fellows, and yes, I was cognizant of the fact that my office trash was removed daily (I had come from my first job at the dynamic yet cash-strapped University of California system—I noticed these small details). Sitting in a lovely conference room for an entire day added to a sense of wistfulness for duty-free intellectual luxuries soon to disappear.

There was also a beauty to each and every delivery along with something concrete to which listeners could relate. For example, as I listened to Arthur Kleinman talk about how leading his ailing wife through the mundane tasks of morning care brought him to consider the "divided self" in new ways, I was one moment moved to tears, the next harrumphing to myself, examining in freeze-frame the flurry of activities that comprise mundane child caregiving—the scramble at the breakfast table to finish last-night's homework, the quick-at-the-sink-teeth-brushing, the bus-stop drops (unless sniffles and fever keep them at home)—that accompany so many women's labors to get careers on track, let alone keep them chugging along at a decent pace. All of these reactions were subtended by a sense of grudging admiration for a long marriage and partnership that has endured up to and through the harrowing changes of Alzheimer's. Other talks were similarly evocative of shared experience: Lila Abu-Lughod began by recounting a visit to Egypt during which she learned that an important father-figure and field informant had recently been incapacitated by stroke. She poignantly described what would be her last visit with a man who had been formative in her life. Whether it was Veena Das' field informant, Billu, whose possibilities were shaped, again, by life and death situations, or Charles Hallisey's musings about his aging mother, or Michael Puett's ancient Chinese philosophers facing the chaos of living—the speakers foregrounded the complexities of human relationships as an emotive hook that then reeled us up to the next level of intellectual analysis.

Yes, I felt drawn into these poignant narrative re-tellings of human experiences. But as an academic, I also recognized that we were not intended to remain, with tissues in hand, at the level of sentiment. Rather, each speaker then stepped back to link experiences of being immersed in the human mundane to larger philosophical projects of "rethinking." As I sat in the Sperry Room, I considered a long durée of rhetorical practices aimed at transforming both selves and worlds. The instinct to create an emotive state conducive to conceptual labor—the affective call for an intellectual response—has deep historical roots. I recognized the structure as one belonging to Christian meditative practice, particularly the Ignatian *Spiritual Exercises*, which I study in their early modern Mexican instantiation.[4] The Jesuits formulated a worldview in which techniques of self-reform were practiced with an eye to reforming the world. The first step toward transformation was compunction: literally, the wounding of the heart that would then lead one to a rationalized re-evaluation of both self and the world. But the Jesuits simply drew upon techniques of the self that had been fine-tuned over centuries of monastic practice. The monastics, in turn, had borrowed unabashedly from Greco-Roman traditions. These practices have established a ground that is both shifting and continuous, a tectonics of affective ritual in which we utilize the mundane in an attempt to build something new, and, importantly, despite the geographical location of the everyday that we consider (whether a Delhi slum or a Cambridge kitchen), the distillation process itself takes place in locations of privilege like the Sperry Room.

In this essay, I want to keep a sharp eye on the multiple locales that the essays and their authors inhabit: the conference room in which the papers were read; the time in which they were written ("our times"); and, finally, the space of memory articulated diachronically, or, more simply, the snippets of intense intersubjective experience recalled from a chronology of years working in field and archive.

Given that temporality underlies these articulations of accumulated individualized experience, it seems appropriate to allow the recently deceased Claude Lévi-Strauss to weigh in—not only because news of his death arrived as I finished this essay—but mostly because he wrote so beautifully on the nature of projecting oneself backward in time. Lévi-Strauss, the prominent French anthropologist and ethnologist, appreciated the way that narratives emerge in broken form through time. At the age of fifty-four in 1955, he published his reflections upon his anthropological career as the book *Tristes Tropiques*. "Time," he wrote, ". . . has extended its isthmus between life and myself; twenty years of forgetfulness were required before I could establish communion with my earlier experience, which I had sought the world over without understanding its significance or appreciating its essence."[5] Many of our essayists are also at a stage of life and career that elicits a kind of reflection on "the human" similar to that which Lévi-Strauss described when contemplating his experiences in the field: "Sharp edges have been blunted and whole sections have collapsed: periods and places collide, are juxtaposed or are inverted, like strata displaced by the tremors on the crust of an ageing planet."[6] Paraphrasing Hallisey, what marvelous tale would Lévi-Strauss have cobbled together forty years beyond *Tristes Tropiques*; what might he have written as a man of ninety?

Perhaps for these essays, it is more accurate to refer to "time, the destroyer, [that] has begun to pile up rubble."[7] Whether haunted by the chronology of a life shared with a wife whose mind is crumbling under the weight of Alzheimer's, the memories called forth by the illness and death of a beloved father figure/field informant, the impossibility of gathering more than a glimmer of understanding of the inner life of one's elderly mother, the desperate choices facing an impoverished brother when a sibling needs a liver transplant, or the hope of ritualized patterning to bring order to natural chaos and death—all of the essayists grapple with existential basics of life and death. Yet the question remains, as scholars sort through the rubble of their own lives and that of their informants, what can be known? What purchase do these exercises have for our rethinking of "the human"?

Temporality

My attempts to form an answer start with themes introduced by the conference keynote speaker, Homi Bhabha, the distinguished postcolonial literary theorist. Bhabha, whose paper could not be included here as it is part of a forthcoming book, set the tone with an address meditating upon what he called the "barbaric transmission of culture," in which he mused on past/present/future—themes related to temporality—in order to insist that we ought not only recognize, but also *inhabit* our moment. Inspired, in part, by Derrida's notion of "messianicity without messianism," Bhabha characterized our time as one of endlessness.[8] For Derrida (the French philosopher and deconstructionist), *messianicity* refers to a future-oriented experience of time that nonetheless refuses to name that future. Derrida carefully explicates this notion as being without hope, but not hopeless, "Not hopeless, in despair, but foreign to the teleology, the hopefulness, and the *salut* of salvation." Derrida further explains messianicity as "heterogeneous and rebellious, irreducible, to law, to power, and to the economy of redemption."[9] As in Derrida, each of the essay writers situates the future-possible in the everyday and refuses the ease of salvation.

Bhabha transposes Derrida's future-possible into a more foreboding key. Bhabha situates us within a chronoscape of "quotidian endlessness" marked by a discourse of continuous war in which an "indeterminate future" weighs heavily. We are waiting. "This agonizing messianism, this messianic moment that is absolutely part of the examination of the here and now as a form of time in which any appeal to the future comes to be nested"[10]—thus, Bhabha, along with the essayists of this volume, insists on the everydayness of a somber and sobering temporality. His first literary example is a moody one: he illustrates this excruciating waiting through Ian McEwan's dark novel *Saturday*, where the rhythm of the plotline beats alternately between lilting anticipation (of a shared family meal) and full-scale dread (of violent death). Barbarism and civility exist side-by-side.

But when Bhabha turns to T.S. Eliot's *Four Quartets*, he sees barbarism and civility not operating in parallel, but conjoined and reconfigured into a productive ambivalence. To situate us in this temporality of "anguish and anticipation, promise and threat," Bhabha hones in on the global imaginary at work in Eliot's poem, the poet's references to "the shores of Asia" and to "Edgeware Road"—a sense of crisis encompassing nation and globe. Bhabha refers us to Eliot to obtain greater comprehension of what it might mean to wait in the present,

> . . . to apprehend
> The point of intersection of the timeless
> With time, is an occupation for the saint.[11]

I emphasize this phrase because it illuminates (despite the reference to saintly occupation) what Derrida means by "messianicity without messianism"—in other words, what it means to hope outside an economy of redemption. But it also serves my purposes to emphasize this *occupation* of the saint. The struggle to apprehend such an "intersection of the timeless with time" is in fact the kind of philosophical practice that the authors in this collection undertake. For social scientists and other investigators, the seemingly timeless human condition is in fact only accessible in time. In the first of the *Four Quartets*, "Burnt Norton," T.S. Eliot calls that intersection between timelessness and time the "still point:"

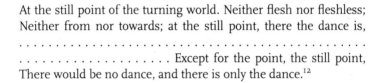

At the still point of the turning world. Neither flesh nor fleshless; Neither from nor towards; at the still point, there the dance is, ... Except for the point, the still point, There would be no dance, and there is only the dance.[12]

Messianicity can be understood as the dance implying a yearned-for but unattainable future-possible that must be worked toward differently in each moment, in each context, in each here-and-now. What does that ambivalence *produce*? Bhabha's answer: "It is by working through or living through the process of ambivalence, its tensions and contentions, that we derive a more appropriate if agonizing measure of global ethical and political conflicts. . . . Ambivalence fosters a vigilant ethics of process and procedure, of partiality and agency, of means and mediation."[13] Here Bhabha signals that we ought to be vigilant for a "still point" that offers no peace or resolution. Ambivalence attends to the present without concrete expectations.

Bhabha's reflections on residing in our twenty-first century resonate deeply with the contributions to this volume. Although Bhabha does not use these terms himself, inhabiting this "agonizing ambivalence" is a form of spiritual exercise. Like Bhabha, the contributors to this volume attend to the present, while attuned to unknown possibilities of transformation. They examine human relationships in an effort to lean toward a horizon impossible to see that Veena Das calls an "eventual everyday." Thus, these essays inflected by the personal are less "confessional" than representative of what contemporary French philosopher Pierre Hadot calls "philosophy as a way of life."[14]

Philosophy of the Concrete

Before I discuss how the essays in this collection might be enriched by considering Hadot's work on spiritual practices, I would like to return to Lévi-Strauss and consider some of his ideas about the structure of knowledge. He eschewed utilitarian notions of knowledge production. Humans do not learn about or engage with the material world because such "things" are deemed useful. Rather, he insisted, we find things "useful or interesting because they are first of all known."[15] In other words, we engage with material as we find it in front of us. Lévi-Strauss called this the "science of the concrete," a radical notion because it leveled the playing field: all humans rely upon methods of observation and reflection.[16] He utilized the language of science to expand the concept of what such a "science" of the concrete might be, differentiating between the layman and the professional using the term "bricoleur" to refer to the former. The French verb bricoler has the sense of puttering, hands-on; current French uses the noun bricolage as Americans use "do-it-yourself." Although our contributors would probably eschew the positivism connoted by "science" (let alone one that is universal), the essays in this volume are very much engaged with the concrete.

Lévi-Strauss contrasted "bricoleurs" with engineers. In his description,

> The 'bricoleur' is adept at performing a large number of diverse tasks . . . His universe of instruments is closed and the rules of his game are always to make do with 'whatever is at hand', that is to say with a set of tools and materials which is always finite and is also heterogeneous because what it contains bears no relation to the current project, or indeed to any particular project, but is the contingent result of all occasions that have been to renew or enrich the stock or to maintain it with the remains of previous constructions or destructions.[17]

He draws an analogy between bricolage and mythical thought, calling mythical thought an "intellectual bricolage," because

> . . . mythical thought . . . expresses itself by means of a heteregenous repertoire, which, even if extensive, is nevertheless limited. It has to use this repertoire, however, whatever the task in hand, because there is nothing else at its disposal.[18]

He later continues this analogy, "Mythical thought for its part is imprisoned in the events and experiences it never tires of ordering and re-ordering in its search to find them a meaning."[19] Yet despite the limited material at hand, mythical thought is expansive, because within it, nothing is meaningless, everything has some potential utility for the *bricoleuse*, who makes something of the pieces she confronts in her everyday.[20] The task of "rethinking the human" is, in fact, an engagement with mythical thought.

Lévi-Strauss, were he to adopt Hadot's terms, might call this the "art of living," the phrase ancient philosophers used to characterize what we often (but not always) do in classrooms and conference rooms. We aim to understand "self" or experience in relation to a cosmic whole, in which the pursuit of knowledge is an exercise in understanding one's path toward (unattainable) wisdom.

Hadot's broad notion of philosophical spiritual exercises conceives them as practices that care for "self" and for "world." In the context of my own research on Ignatian spirituality, I often think about this expanded category of "spiritual exercises." I appreciate Pierre Hadot's work because he makes an important de-Christianizing (although not de-Westernizing) move when he explores the roots of these exercises in the world of Greco-Roman elites. He provides a general definition of spiritual exercises:

> . . . these exercises have as their goal the transformation of our vision of the world, and the metamorphosis of our being. They therefore have not merely moral, but also an existential value. We are not just dealing here with a code of good moral conduct, but with a way of being, in the strongest sense of the term.[21]

Instructions in the "art of living" linked notions of "self"[22] to a *process* of understanding of one's place in the cosmic whole.[23] They emphasized understanding one's place on a path toward perfection, rather than perfect knowledge. Within this quest, knowledge of physics, for example, could be considered crucial to practicing philosophy as a way of life because particular knowledge of the lived environment allowed one to seek to transcend it.[24] This strikes me as a particularly apt way to frame many of the contributions to this collection. These essayists' contemplation of the particular simultaneously *invokes* and *questions* Western universals.

Yet Hadot's invocation of the universal seems to run counter to the insistence on the "still point" or the agonizing ambivalence, within which these authors labor to reside. I have insisted on the two spaces of production—the field and the Sperry Room—because I wanted to maintain the intersubjective and the academic-performative as discrete spaces in tension with one another. Invoking Hadot illuminates another layer of ambivalence born of residing in both spaces, of speaking from the Western tradition even while seeking to find our way out of it. This is not a new insight: it has been the terrain of postcolonial criticism for well over a decade. Hadot helps us to see the problem framed a bit differently. But does Hadot's notion of care for self and world—a legacy I am convinced our contributors take part in—leave universals as too static, unchanging and—most troublesome—stubbornly Western? Hadot writes: "In other words, caring for ourselves and questioning ourselves occur only when our individuality is transcended and we rise to the level of universality . . ."[25]

While I find Hadot very useful for thinking through these essays, I want to interrogate his vision of "spiritual exercises" by re-reading him alongside Lévi-Strauss' *Savage Mind*. The collective goal for our essay writers is not transcendence or salvation, but rather to experiment with methodologies for residing in the tensions of agonizing ambivalence. To transpose into Lévi-Strauss' terms, we might call them primitive philosophers[26] because they eschew the aims of a transcendent social science and rather, have embraced the role of the *bricoleur*, whose making and remaking with fragments that "come in handy"[27] claims a stake in a philosophy that has always been a way of life.

For these scholars, philosophy resides somewhere between the laborious observation of data collection and the fleeting moments of inspiration. Lévi-Strauss knew this well, as he wrote, "I have learnt that the truth of a situation is to be found not in day-to-day observation but in the patient and piecemeal process of distillation." Lévi-Strauss' process of distillation is, in fact, the undertaking that, as I have sketched above, Bhabha, Derrida, Hadot, and Eliot all call us to: caught in the web of history, of hope, we inhabit the present but also embody the past. From this space, Lévi-Strauss draws our attention to the role of the fragmentary in the process of distillation. "Exploration," he writes, "is not so much a covering of surface distance but as a study in depth: a fleeting episode, a fragment of landscape or a remark overheard may provide the only means of understanding and interpreting areas which would otherwise remain barren of meaning."[28]

Bricolage

Arthur Kleinman, to borrow words from Veena Das' essay which follows his, has become "awake to life" through the practice of caring for his ailing wife. Caregiving itself is his interlocutor: the tender care of his wife is the existential ground of his inquiry into the human. In his essay, Kleinman ruminates on how the abstract is anchored in concreteness of the everyday. Putting the paper towel in his wife's hand to dry a single dish is a cultivation of humanity, the work of the everyday against her "unraveling brain structure" includes her in the quotidian rituals that rebuild their relationship on new terrain, a terrain now missing shared memories. Kleinman's caregiving exemplifies the philosophy of the concrete. Like Lévi-Strauss, he sees our immediate environment as calling humans to action, as compelling him to engage with the tasks at hand. He draws us into the mundane activities that comprise caring for another human body—feeding, bathing, dressing—duties that call him to be present. He explores how "presence" demands alertness and engagement, not only as a conscious decision but also as an embodied reaction to those concrete tasks.

Veena Das writes here about how encounters with others can re-order everyday life and awaken us to our lives. The experiences of her informant, Billu, took shape in relation to the illnesses of his brother and his newborn children. Through Billu, we see death (or ill health) mediated by two outside "others," medical technology (the possibility of a transplant for Billu's brother) and the occult world (the demands made by a spirit, the Lady in White). Both demand regimes of care (attention to village life, for example, by the Lady in White, who later demands that he care for his child) while attention to money and to institutional norms is demanded by the medical world to which Billu is required (but not always able) to attend. Das' analysis of Billu's engagement with the everyday brings her to an important critique of morality as defined in terms of "the transcendental." She suggests "the eventual everyday" as a horizon—a potentiality—that might substitute for "universal" or "transcendental" morality.

In a lovely and lyrical essay that explores the accumulation of knowledge and experience over time, Charles Hallisey contemplates the impossibilities of knowing another, pointing out, "We experience the experience of aging in different ways over the course of our lifetimes." Hallisey's reflections upon his mother's aging from what he calls the position of "seeing sideways" is an exercise in seeking to know what cannot be known. The practice itself is important, he writes, because it is "leading on towards"—a phrase that deliberately has no object. Hallisey also points to the singularity of human experience when he asks, what can be known about a woman at ninety—"especially if one loves her"? He takes this latter line from Adorno, to emphasize how love has us see differently. He is also inspired by Adorno's concept of "late style"—an artist's ability to find beauty in the discordant. From Buddhist thought, Hallisey introduces the concept of *jinen*, which he translates as "made to become so." Like Kleinman's comment that we are not born fully human, and similar to the way that Eliot used the German *erhebung* to describe a state of uplifted suspension, humans are "made to become so." Aging, like *jinen*, "seems to reach us from the outside and we cannot grasp it." Hallisey's ambivalent spiritual exercise inhabits and finds beauty in the discordance of a continuity that is also transformation—but never fully graspable as either or both. The phrases "made to become so," "lead on towards," and "to see sideways" provide movement toward a future-possible, and make available a useful vocabulary for meditations on an eventual everyday.

Like Hallisey, Lila Abu-Lughod articulates the role that love plays in singular moments of intersubjectivity, or, as she refers to them, as moments of "bridging." The roles she inhabited as mother, feminist, traveler, and "loved and loving" befriended "daughter" in a Bedouin family form the foundation for her critique of the Western universals deployed in human rights discourse. Abu-Lughod's role as a special daughter in a Bedouin family allowed her to bridge their different worlds. The Haj was the interlocutor that brought Abu-Lughod to take up ambivalence as a philosophical stance, for her practice of tactical humanism is a philosophical exercise that asks us not to merely translate across experience, but instead to build and rebuild bridges through a practice of continually acting toward the unattainable. Accordingly, she considers "family" as a model for bridging individual difference, a model that accounts for both love and dysfunction. Her ethnographic description examines not only cognitive exchange, but also the gestures that comprise embodied communication, including those that indicated the love of a family patriarch for his foreign daughter. From the space of this familial relationship lived through time, her essay—both poignant and trenchant—challenges us to develop our thinking about kinship as a model that would step outside the problematic dyad of "universal/particular." Instead, Abu-Lughod pushes toward a more complex engagement with particulars that takes into consideration both the genealogy of their production (global-historical forces) as well as their philosophical deployment: the "family" as an ambivalent model for meditating upon an eventual everyday.

Michael Puett's contribution to this volume offers an intriguing intellectual exercise that might be conceived as a counterpoint to Chakrabarty's call to provincialize.[29] Theory is useful, Puett suggests, but must it be Western theory? He self-consciously constructs a theory of humanity by taking fourth and third century BCE Chinese particulars which he transposes into a universal theory about human ritual process. In his re-reading of Xunxi and Mencius, Puett finds a ritual practice of patterned re-ordering in an effort to temporarily transform the fragmented conditions of the everyday. Homi Bhabha's chronotype of "endlessness" pervades Puett's theory-making: "The attempt to place the world into a set of patterned relationships, in short, is a never-ending project," Puett writes, "the domestication of the world is never complete." Puett identifies the universal philosophical impulses that animate ritual tradition, but self-consciously foregrounds the temporary and fragmentary results of such actions. Indeed, there is no transcending negative impulses, just the endless task of creating and re-creating patterns out of "the fundamentally fractured and fragmented" nature of humanity. "The problem for humans is to begin the process—and it will never end—of trying to create connections and build out from this fragmented world a more ethical world."

Conclusion

In Puett's construction, making and remaking one's world is a philosophical practice that humans need to undertake. Here again, the echoes of Lévi-Strauss' "science of the concrete" resound. It is only a small step from here to interpret the papers themselves as philosophical exercises of making and remaking selves in relation to concrete others in an effort to make (and remake) a world. In its broadest form, the notion of philosophical or spiritual exercises captures not only the process of ordering both self and world, but also something of the ritual import of presenting these ruminations in the Sperry Room. Homi Bhabha called for "a vigilant ethics of process and procedure, of partiality and agency, of means and mediation."[30] His word is "mediation," but this ethics also offers itself as a form of *meditation*, a secular or academic spiritual exercise that produces what Aaron Stalnaker has referred to as "chastened intellectualism."[31]

Each author's narrative wrestles with dominant Western scholarly universals. Yet to "provincialize" European hegemonic discourses does not necessarily dismantle them. The problem, as Dipesh Chakrabarty knows too well, is inescapable, " 'Europe' cannot after all be provincialized within the institutional site of the university," he writes, pointing out how the globality of academia is linked to the history of the imposition of Western modernity.[32] Every attempt to dismantle Western theoretical traditions runs the risk of replicating them. As Bruno Latour notes dryly, "To unmask: that was our sacred task, the task of us moderns. To reveal the true calculations underlying the false consciousnesses, or the true interests underlying the false calculations. Who is not still foaming slightly at the mouth with that particular rabies?"[33]

Does Latour describe a feedback loop that remains ultimately inescapable? In linking what academics do in the field and in conference rooms to philosophical practices that reach back to the ancient Greeks and Romans, am I arguing that we remain unable to escape the ultimate omnivore of the Western intellectual tradition? I hesitate to launch such a critique at the authors in this collection who are so wholly devoted to residing in that particular tension. They do not move to swift synthesis; rather, they embrace the contradictions and find beauty in the discord inherent in using the tools of Western academic disciplines to effect a dismantling of Western universals, a dismantling that is never more than a gesture that reshapes, reconstructs and reconfigures human experience within the Western intellectual tradition that, yes, is the ultimate omnivore.

Yet, in keeping with Puett, we keep doing and redoing, drawing upon the concrete everyday to create anew. As an act of being vigilant over thought and intention, writing and thinking about "the human" can be the means by which we not only link the mud and dust-covered facts from archive and field to a meaningful vision, but by which we order our everyday. We are *bricoleurs*, we are myth-makers, putting order to the fragmentary nature of the rubble that forms our lives.

NOTES

1. A word of thanks to my co-editor, Don Swearer, and to all the contributors. It was a pleasure to edit these dazzling essays. For careful readings and critical comments, I am indebted to Kristi Keuhn, Robert Orsi, and Cristie Traina. Thanks to my WSRP colleague Miryam Segal who read and commented on this in its many instantiations. Particular gratitude must be expressed to Victor Pimstein who bought *Tristes Tropiques* for me just two days before Lévi-Strauss passed away. Finally, I am extremely grateful for the experience of working with Susan Lloyd McGarry, a phenomenal editor and writer from whom I learned so much.

2. Michael Jackson, *Minima Ethnographica: Intersubjectivity and the Anthropological Project* (Chicago: University of Chicago Press, 1998), 12.

3. See Clifford Geertz, "Deep Play: Notes on the Balinese Cockfight" in *The Interpretation of Culture* (New York: Basic Books, 1973), 412–454.

4. See, for example, J. Michelle Molina, "Technologies of the Self: Letters of Eighteenth-Century Mexican Jesuit Spiritual Daughters," *History of Religions* 47:4 (May 2008): 282–303.

5. Claude Lévi-Strauss, *Tristes Tropiques*, trans. John and Doreen Weightman (New York: Penguin Books, paperback, 1973), 44.

6. Ibid.

7. Ibid.

8. Homi K. Bhabha, keynote address at conference "Rethinking the Human," May 12, 2008, Center for the Study of World Religions at Harvard Divinity School. Unpublished transcript. Video of the talk available online at http://www.hds.harvard.edu/cswr/resources/lectures/bhabha.html. These ideas will be expanded in his forthcoming book from Harvard University Press, "A Measure of Dwelling."

9. Jacques Derrida, *Rogues: Two Essays on Reason*, trans. Pascale-Anne Brault and Michael Naas (Stanford: Stanford University Press, 2005), xv.

10. Bhabha, Transcript, 17.

11. T.S. Eliot, "The Dry Salvages" in *Four Quartets* (Florida: Harcourt-Brace, 1973 reprint), 45, 46.

12. T.S. Eliot, "Burnt Norton" in *Four Quartets*, 16.

13. Bhabha, Transcript, 37.

14. See Pierre Hadot, *Philosophy as a Way of Life: Spiritual Exercises from Socrates to Foucault*, ed. Arnold Davidson, trans. Michael Chase (Malden, MA: Blackwell, 1995).

15. Claude Lévi-Strauss, *The Savage Mind* (Chicago: University of Chicago Press, 1966), 9.

16. Lévi-Strauss, *Savage Mind*, the first chapter is called "The Science of the Concrete," 1–34.

17. Ibid., 17.

18. Ibid.

19. Ibid., 22.

20. Ibid.
21. Hadot, *Philosophy as a Way of Life*, 127. See 86–87 for descriptions of the very different spiritual exercises of the Stoics and the Epicureans.
22. Notions of "self" are quite different in Hellenistic thought and should not be conflated with the modern "I." In contrast to a Cartesian or Augustinian self, the ancient self was comprehended more in terms of a "he" than an "I." Arnold Davidson, "Ethics as Ascetics: Foucault, the History of Ethics, and Ancient Thought," in *Foucault and the Writing of History*, ed. Jan Goldstein (Oxford, UK: Blackwell, 1994), 74.
23. Hadot, *Philosophy as a Way of Life*, 83.
24. Ibid., 87.
25. Pierre Hadot, *What is Ancient Philosophy?*, trans. Michael Chase (Cambridge: Harvard University Press, 2002), 32.
26. Lévi-Strauss suggests that in describing the science of the concrete we use the term "prior" rather than "primitive." Lévi-Strauss, *Savage Mind*, 16.
27. Lévi-Strauss, *Savage Mind*, 18.
28. Lévi-Strauss, *Tristes Tropiques*, 47–48.
29. Dipesh Chakrabarty, *Provincializing Europe: Postcolonial Thought and Historical Difference* (Princeton: Princeton University Press, 2000). As well as his overarching call to contest the global universal, Chakrabarty examines another divide relevant to this book: that between analytic and hermeneutic traditions in the social sciences, with the forefathers of each being Marx and Heidegger respectively (see 18). The essays in this book could be seen as coming mostly from the hermeneutic tradition.
30. Bhabha, Transcript, 37.
31. See Aaron Stalnaker, *Overcoming our Evil: Human Nature and Spiritual Exercises in Xunzi and Augustine* (Washington, DC: Georgetown University Press, 2006), particularly 275-287. In this book Stalnaker examines some of the same texts as Puett, but for different ends.
32. Chakrabarty, *Provincializing Europe*, 45–46.
33. Bruno Latour, *We Have Never Been Modern*, trans. Catherine Porter (Cambridge: Harvard University Press, 1993), 44.

Caregiving: The Divided Meaning of Being Human and the Divided Self of the Caregiver

Arthur Kleinman

Introduction

Caregiving is simultaneously two very different things. On one side, it burdens our resources, divides our emotions, intensifies interpersonal conflicts, and opposes our deepest aspirations against what matters in giving (and receiving) care. Caregiving can make us feel frustrated and desperate. On the other side (and there is always this other side), being a caregiver, especially caregiving for those with severe illness and disabilities, can make us feel more responsible and meaningful. Caregiving can enhance our compassion, solicit solidarity, and elicit a fuller, more human presence than we ever realized we possessed. Caregiving intensifies our conscious sense of being pulled in conflicting directions; by tapping into our latent tensions, it brings unconscious and embodied conflicts into play. The upshot is a clearer picture of our divided condition as the human condition.

The Western intellectual tradition is filled with examples of writers who have regarded the self to be divided: observing and doing; ego/id/superego; the borderland between the normal and the pathological; spiritual and materialistic; pragmatic and ideological; built out of contradictions and opposition; and so on. Many cultural traditions, including the Chinese, regard human nature to be both good and bad. Local worlds—our moral context—contain conflicts between what is at stake for individuals and what is at stake for the group. Caregiving, founded in this basic division of human experience, exposes troubling truths about what it means to be human. First, we are not born fully human, nor do we naturally become so. Our condition is not only divided, but incomplete, as Henry James wrote, ". . . everyone, in life, is incomplete . . . ."[1] We are called by fated circumstances to be there for others, to respond to others' needs. Through the practice of caregiving, we become aware of our incompleteness and the limits of our selfhood. Only then through the demanding practice of caregiving do we begin to realize the fullness of our humanity, as well as the limits of our capability to transcend the self and develop the interpersonal moral potential of what it means to be human. What starts out as caregiving for others becomes caregiving for ourselves. The incompleteness and limitations in caregiving are also inherent in being human and suggest the paradox that becoming more human also means becoming more fully aware of contradiction, failure, and incompleteness in our own lives. Realizing the human, then, is not so much an uplifting story as it is a critical and deep soberness over the fate and destiny of humanity and ourselves.

Nonetheless, when viewed at the collective, societal level, caregiving is among those usually hidden pro-social activities of everyday life keeping the world going. It is difficult to imagine a world without caregiving, just as it is hard to imagine a world without love. The actions of caregiving create the emotional foundations for solidarity, for sustaining responsibility. Through caregiving, I have experienced a radical transformation in myself. I have come to sympathies and empathies which I understood intellectually, but did not possess in an embodied sense. Part of the reason that these pro-social activities remain hidden is that caregiving so often falls to women, immigrants, and the poor in our society.

Homi Bhaba reminds us that the transmission of barbarism, as well as the transmission and cultivation of humanness, often comes in small acts—and sometimes together in the same act.[2] It is not just that the reality of concentration camps, killing fields, and the "grey zone" of predatory local worlds tells us that caregiving is fragile and can be negated. In a quieter way, indifference to and, at worst, abandonment of the seriously impaired by family and professionals through denial and avoidance of human needs tells us much the same thing. Caregiving needs to be sustained in the face of such very real threats as poverty, war, stigma, and indifference.

To truly understand caregiving, we must have a feel for the concrete practices that protect and sustain carereceivers on a daily basis. It is not enough to superficially list practices such as feeding, bathing, toileting, and dressing sick and disabled family members and close friends. Only through actually carrying out intimate caregiving practices do we learn to be caregivers. This tacit, embodied, time-dependent knowledge requires us to feel, smell, see, and live with pain, suffering, and physical and mental limitation. The concrete everyday reinforces the stubbornness of things, the way our environment can compel us to engage with what is directly in front of us, forcing us to be present. Embodied knowledge requires us to roll up our sleeves and get dirty, tired, and frustrated; yet for all that, we feel more human: both more present and more divided.

While I have written this essay with a very specific experience of everyday caregiving in mind, the world of professional medicine is also on the horizon of my thoughts. The very practices that constitute caregiving among family members and friends also reveal why health professionals are often so limited in their caregiving, and why merely teaching about caregiving in professional schools, in the absence of actually doing it, is unlikely to improve this existential craft for professionals. Professionals of all types simply do not have enough at stake in their relations with patients, parishioners, and clients to invest themselves into their caregiving practices. Moreover, institutional settings further limit the experience of professionals, impairing them from bringing the fullness of their presence into interactions with patients and families. Yet there are health professionals who do, showing it can be done. Contrary to cultural expectations that emphasize caregiving as either burden *or* love, frustration *or* compassion, in my experience, when caregivers feel sufficiently empowered to reveal their own divided experience (the self divided between burden *and* compassion), this disclosure facilitates (rather than undermines) their caregiving.

The Practices of Caregiving

It is between 6 and 6:30 AM on a frigid New England morning. I (the caregiver) wake my wife of forty-four years, Joan Kleinman (the carereceiver), and lead her by hand into the bathroom. (I have already taken her there at 2 AM and 5 AM). Joan has suffered from an atypical form of Alzheimer's disease for six years now. The disease has made her functionally blind and disoriented, unable to find her way around the house we have lived in for twenty-seven years. It has also cratered her memory, making a ruin of thought, feeling, and the taken-for-granted skill of relating to others. I have to assist her in finding and sitting on the toilet, cleaning herself, washing her face and hands, and drying them with a towel. I lead her to the bath that I have drawn, hand her the soap, help her get in and out, and give her a towel. I lead her back into our bedroom and help her remove her bathrobe. I hand her face cream to put on, give her the underarm deodorant. I choose what she will wear and dress her. I slip the brassiere straps over her arms and snap it closed. I give her new panties and hold her shoulders while she balances herself to put them on. I put on her tights. I pull the sweater over her head and arms, and hand her a brush for her hair. It has taken me thirty minutes to help my wife do these things, and now I need to take a bath, shave, and dress. When that is done, I lead Joan by the hand into the kitchen, place her in a chair, and make breakfast. The Darjeeling tea glows hot and golden red in the cup. "Wonderful," she whispers. I place a fork in her right hand and guide it to the poached eggs in the bowl. After eating I wash our dishes. The scalding water is always a surprise, yet it's comforting. I hand her a paper towel and a dish to dry. She smiles with pleasure as she wipes the plate dry, then hands it shakily to me to put away in the cupboard.³ Afterward I make sure she takes her pills, brushes her teeth, and goes to the toilet again.

Some mornings go smoothly; some are more trying. Joan is usually happy and interactive; but some days she is apathetic and others agitated. Her agitation not infrequently makes me anxious. Like anxiety, anger is also contagious. There are many occasions for the spiraling dynamics of these primary affects, as well as for sadness, frustration, resignation, and resistance.

By 9 AM on weekdays, when our helpful home health aide arrives, I am ready to depart for work: often tired, sometimes annoyed, frequently frustrated, but not infrequently buoyed with a feeling of having accomplished something crucial. I am there for Joan, and she elicits from me all the warmth and affection I can muster. I am fully alive when I am with her. She responds to that vital connection with all the humanness she can still express. My feelings and thoughts may be divided along the lines of being burdened versus feeling exalted by what I am called to do, but the reality is that of performing very concrete actions. It is the performance of these highly specific practices that makes me a caregiver. I do it, not based on rational choices but because it is there to do, and I am called by everything in our relationship to do it.

The practices I engage in are not performed perfunctorily or mechanically. I am as fully alive while carrying them out as I am at any moment of real significance. They are bodily movements, but they are also meanings, emotions, and moral experiences. Here moral means what is at stake for me and for her. Caring for Joan matters greatly for me, as it does for her. But it is not all that is at stake for us; sometimes we are divided over other essentials that matter. After all, we have children, grandchildren, work, dreams, and other responsibilities and relationships. We may be in or out of sync with ourselves and with each other. But our divided selves only deepen and make our relationship more complex and important. Yes, we are caregiver and carereceiver; but we are also husband and wife, research collaborators, parents and grandparents, lovers, financial partners, religious participants, etc. While caregiving must now be a central component in our lives, it is interlaced with others in a rich stew of embodied, intersubjective, and moral entanglements. A shared narrative and sensibility sustains those entanglements; yet, they too are rarefying and becoming something else over the course of caregiving.

My preferred means for evoking our caregiving relationship is the idea of *presence*.

Presence

I remember vividly the excitement I felt when Joan and I first met at a French film series at Stanford in 1964. That excitement brought forth from each of us liveliness and passion. Minutes were full of our being for and with each other. Call it love. Over the years, it deepened and burnished. It also became entangled with our divided selves—distinctive academic aspirations, self-critical reflections, feelings for others. These in turn merged with shared narratives and sensibilities to make our presence for each other more complex and enduring.

Anthropologists of religion set out core cross-cultural elements in religious practice, including, among others, theodicy, ritual, embodiment, sacred spaces (and the pilgrimages to them), transformative power, and presence. By presence, such anthropologists generally mean the experience of divinity being present in a ritual and in sacred space for the participants, and reciprocally, the participant being present for the divine.[4] Presence also carries with it the idea of being there in the fullness of one's being, as in the biblical phrase: "Here I am, Lord," or in the experience of *darsan* in Hindu pilgrimages to sacred sites. *Darsan* implies an ability to see the everyday transformed into miraculous acts of sight and communion with the divine, through which spiritual reality, either positive or negative, can be revealed.[5] This idea of presence calls to mind sense of being avid as well as alert, attentive and ready, responsible, and actively engaged.

Perhaps the pivotal universal human experience that evokes presence is suffering—suffering by the afflicted, their families, and their social networks. Indeed, the universality of suffering grants it central importance in all major world religions, and all religions have some mechanism for coping with suffering.[6] All Christian traditions have recourse to prayer, either in personal or group settings, to mediate suffering. In the early

Christian church, suffering was viewed as a salvation of sorts by bringing one closer to the experience of Christ[7] or uniting the divided self through pain that affected both the physical and spiritual realms. In contemporary times, both pastoral and lay care is important in coping with suffering resulting from ill health.[8]

On a more mundane plane, each of us has the experience of being present for others, meaning that we feel intensely alive and committed, and we are participating fully in an emotional and practical sense. Love or charisma or other elements in our relations with others call forth our presence, but other elements and our responses to them, such as fear or shame, deter or prevent us from being fully present. We are far more likely to be present in domestic settings than in work settings, where technical rationality, routinization, and other aspects of bureaucracy push us into role relations and professional distance. Moreover, the same people or setting can call forth as well as suppress the presence of an individual on different occasions. Think of how our responses can differ from day to day because of changes in mood, conversation, the issues at hand, and our coping skills (or lack thereof).

Caregiving in the space of our homes is far more likely to call forth presence than caregiving in professional spaces like the ward or clinic. But this is not by any means an absolute divide: we can be present to our patients and not present with family members. Nor does presence map directly on to Weber's division of enchanted and disenchanted worlds.[9] I have seen Taiwanese shamans who were not present to the gods or clients in healing rituals—even their parishioners understood that they were acting perfunctorily, merely going through the motions of possession. I have also known individuals in highly secular spaces who were intensely present to friends and patients. Presence in and of itself is not always associated with good actions. There are well-documented cases of sociopaths and incompetent professionals who were famous for their presence. Nonetheless, presence does mean that the person is fully alive and involved, and that the interpersonal relations he or she animates realize emotional and moral intensity and authenticity.

Caregiving for health catastrophes and serious disabilities can frequently call forth the presence of adult children and other relatives and close friends who are engaged in the actual practices of giving care. That is what makes those practices so greatly human. It is not a matter of changing bed sheets, washing a loved one's face, or feeding an elderly parent as a routinized duty, but that often (in my experience quite often), the ordinary caregiving practice becomes charged with emotional and moral meaning.

Quality caregiving is difficult to accomplish in professional care because practices become routinized and the relationship becomes defined as the professional care of strangers. Yet, just as the home health aide develops a caring relationship that often becomes infused with emotional and moral meanings of friendship, domesticity, and solidarity, so too do clinical relationships over time hold the potential for greater presence and therefore greater humanity.

It is crucial to understand presence in the context of the divided self. Emotional intensity can overwhelm a caregiving relationship. Anger and frustration can undermine caregiving practices. They too are forms of presence. Presence must be understood as containing an element of self-critical reflection. All caregivers have had experiences of being barbaric. The disabled are vulnerable. Engagement is fraught and frustrating. There are moments when you yell.[10] The self is a complex, multisided, divided self. That dark side is there; it can emerge in various ways. The divided self helps in part explain how we can be self-absorbed, self-interested, destructive, unmaking in one set of acts, and remaking, repairing, caregiving in another. Here awareness of the divided self can assure that caregivers, both lay and professional, are not carried away or blinded to the dangers of enmeshment and overinvolvement. Ethics, aesthetics, and religion can help open up cultural spaces that allow room for self-critical reflection.[11]

The divided subjectivity of caregivers, then, is both a limiting fact in creating presence and in overdoing presence. Perhaps we are never completely present, even to ourselves, because one side of us observes, interprets, and introduces irony and self-criticism into experience. And yet, we know when we are present. And we also know the opposite—the failure—when we are called to be present and, despite this call, are still not there for someone.

Much in anthropology has dealt with suffering, but also with violence, trauma, and oppression.[12] The body is viewed as the existential ground of culture, and culture is seen as a projection of the body into the world.[13] In the same way that sick people embody meaning from their social world, so do caregivers. Presence involves embodiment through the intensification of emotion in personhood. Presence also includes the embodiment of the divided self and of divided social worlds in which individuals and the group may have conflicting goals.

In considering the concept of presence in relation to caregiving, we cannot neglect the presence of the carereceiver. Oftentimes, the carereceiver, particularly in cases of Alzheimer's disease and other neurodegenerative conditions, is treated only as a historical presence, interacted with only through memories of who they once were. As memories and abilities are eroded by the course of the disease, caregivers, both lay and professional, can too easily discount the ways that patients can still interact with their world and be present in their own lives. Medical anthropologist Janelle Taylor, in speaking of her mother with Alzheimer's, discusses the emphasis that well-meaning friends and professional caregivers place on recognition by frequently asking if her mother recognizes her. Although Taylor says that her mother does not know her name, she knows her as someone important in her life, recognizing her on a deeper level. Although the tenor of the mother-daughter relationship has drastically changed due to the Alzheimer's, Taylor aptly illustrates how her mother is, in fact, still present in their relationship and how she continues to be an active participant in the time they spend together.[14]

Ethical Implications for the Professions

There are many professionals associated with providing catastrophic and terminal care, including physicians, nurses, social workers, physical and occupational therapists, psychotherapists, and pastoral counselors. I firmly believe that anyone in these helping professions should have the opportunity to practice caregiving and become a primary caregiver in the domestic space of the carereceiver as a part of their training. Actual prolonged experience of caregiving is sharply limited in most professional educational settings. One interesting and important counterexample to this is found at the University of Leiden, Holland, where all first year medical students are required to serve as primary caregivers in patients' homes. Further, the professional ethics taught to students of medicine, nursing, social work, and divinity must include what patients, families and their social networks face with lay caregiving.

From either a religious or nonreligious perspective, the existential reality of caregiving needs to be central to the mission of professional ethical instruction. Ethics are currently taught in such a way that local realities are not considered, yet caregiving takes place in the real world, embedded in the physical, social, and spiritual contexts of people's everyday lives. In her book *Talking with Patients about the Personal Impact of Illness: The Doctor's Role*, Lenore Buckley discusses barriers to empathy on the part of doctors, primarily including: lack of personal experience with serious illness, health system bureaucracy, and the difficulty of switching between professional language with colleagues to a more accessible, empathetic language with patients.[15] These barriers can only be overcome once long-term experience with caregiving is required of those training in the helping professions. There are also, of course, barriers to caregiving for nonprofessional caregivers, aside from those illustrated above in my consideration of the divided self. Financial constraints can create a large barrier, as can lack of access to health services, and difficulty in finding local support, from suitable health aides, family, friends, and neighbors.

Many religious traditions offer a basis for an ethic of care. From a contemporary Christian perspective, Sister Simone Roach argues that caring is the human mode of being and that a return to this central ethic is the only way to rescue professionalized caregiving in Western society. In her view, in order for health professionals to truly be healing, they must be trained not just in the practice of caring but must focus on caring as the basic human affective response to the world.[16] Arguing a similar position from a secular perspective is Joan Tronto, who postulates care as the fundamental ethic of humanity. She holds that this ethic of care is marginalized in modern American society, largely because of the strict separation of morality and politics and the equally strict separation of public and private spheres that relegates care to a private rather than a political realm.[17]

Teaching ethics to professionals requires that we help them develop the ability to move out of and away from the technical rationality of protocols and toward the most human aspects of suffering and healing—aspects that require imagination of damaged subjectivity and suffering families, compassion based in detailed understanding of what the seriously sick and their intimate circle face, and presence. Here presence—being there for those in need, being with them in the experience of illness, being free to express the most human of sentiments in the context of moral commitment and solidarity—may be the fulcrum that swings the professional out of the bureaucratic mode of engagement and into the humanity of the healer. Encouraging students to express their presence and to understand what constrains and what liberates it may be one of the more important elements in ethical training. Similarly, identifying and reducing the major barriers to instating clinical presence may be what ethicists need to contribute to pedagogy and to the reform of professional health care and social welfare systems.

Ethics in the absence of presence is a disembodied, truncated perspective cut off from real action. The *presence* of ethics, however, must also account for the divided conditions that constitute our humanity. It must be a presence that is simultaneously an engaged mode of being-in-the-world and a critical self-reflection on that being and that world.

Hence both aspects of presence must be taught, practiced, evaluated, and supported in the life of the professional. Professional formation and education acts as a model of what is possible, what is expected, and what is human. Including these aspects of presence within professional education can also help to build a repository of experiences and practices that may be transferable to the nonprofessional.

Conclusion

Some years ago, I introduced the idea of social suffering as a means of challenging and refashioning the established separation between social and health problems into domains of medicine, welfare, response to catastrophes, etcetera. The moral, the political, the economic, and the medical so overlap that we need to rethink how we approach human problems. I feel that same way about caregiving. Much of the writing on health care is tired and conventional. It is so preoccupied with economic and technical matters that it overlooks what caregiving is for. We need to rethink caregiving as an existential moral experience. That experience tells us as much about the local moral worlds that encompass us as about our personal stakes and human conditions.

In this paper, I emphasize the divided nature of our human circumstances, which the school of American pragmatism (Dewey, James, et al.)[18] understood to be central to how we live and respond to human problems. By and large, health policy experts, ethicists, even pastoral counselors have failed to consider this divided self and divided world in their analyses. The result is a flat and often irrelevant version of local life that misses what matters most.[19] What happens when we start the analysis with our divided condition? I suggest that it leads to a different way of thinking about caregiving. In turn, that reformulation of this object of inquiry has practical consequences for the reform of health care systems and for the resources available to families. This essay is not the place to move from local experience to policy, but I believe that movement is crucial if families and friendship networks and home health care workers are to receive the resources they require to sustain and enhance the pro-social work of caregiving. Emphasizing the divided self leads to a different pedagogy of caregiving as well as a different ethics of care, all of which are subjects for further consideration and which may help us in rethinking the human.

Most of the technically detailed work in scholarly lives leads us to ultimately dissatisfying and banal statements like "that word needs to be unpacked" or "this discourse needs to be understood." Caregiving is an important topic because the stubbornness of suffering makes us realize there is more in the world than discourse and more for scholarship than discourse. Experience itself is extraordinary ground, not just for novelists and poets and painters but for scholars as well, because it means engaging with the stubbornness of things—the fact that you cannot make cancer or schizophrenia or dementia anything you want by calling up a different perspective or drawing on a different ideology. All our personal and cultural constructions must start in that stubbornness of things. The grounding of experience in the reality of caregiving shows us how practice leads the way into the moral

NOTES

1. Henry James, *Letters, Volume II: 1875–1883*, ed. Leon Edel (Cambridge: Belknap Press of Harvard University Press, 1975), 324. From an 1880 letter to Grace Norton, discussing the heroine of his novel *Portrait of a Lady*.

2. Homi K. Bhabha, "On the Barbaric Transmission of Culture," Paper presented at the conference "Rethinking the Human," May 12, 2008, Center for the Study of World Religions at Harvard Divinity School, Cambridge, MA. Unpublished transcript. Video of the talk available online at http://www.hds.harvard.edu/cswr/resources/lectures/bhabha.html. These ideas will be expanded in his forthcoming book from Harvard University Press, "A Measure of Dwelling."

3. This description of the daily trials of caregiving, paraphrased here, appears at length in a previous article. See Arthur Kleinman, "Caregiving: the odyssey of becoming more human," *The Lancet*, 373:9660 (Jan. 2009): 292–293.

4. See Thomas Csordas, *The Sacred Self: A Cultural Phenomenology of Charismatic Healing* (Berkeley: University of California Press, 1997), and *Embodiment and Experience: The existential ground of culture and self* (Cambridge: Cambridge University Press, 1994).

5. See Diana L. Eck, *Darsan: Seeing the Divine Image in India* (Chambersburg, PA: Anima Books, 1981).

6. See John Bowker, *Problems of Suffering in Religions of the World* (Cambridge: Cambridge University Press, 1970).

7. David J. Melling, "Suffering and Sanctification in Christianity," in *Religion, Health, and Suffering*, ed. John R. Hinnells and Roy Porter (New York: Kegan Paul International, 1999), 46–64.

8. Ibid.

9. See *From Max Weber: Essays in Sociology*, trans. and ed. H. H. Gerth and C. Wright Mills (New York: Oxford University Press, 1946), for a good overview. The idea of "the disenchantment of the world" is discussed in several of Weber's essays in that book, including "Science as a Vocation," 129–156, particularly 155, and "The Social Psychology of the World's Religions," 267–301 and also the introduction, 51.

10. See John Bayley, *Elegy for Iris* (New York: Picador, 1999). This memoir about Bayley's caregiving for his wife, Iris Murdoch, conveys some of the intricacies of caregiving with its accompanying frustrations.

11. For more about the possibilities inherent in the humanities for increasing self-reflection, including further implications for professional medical education and ethics, see Arthur Kleinman, "Catastrophe and Caregiving: the failure of medicine as an art," *The Lancet*, 371:9606, January 2008, 22–23.

12. See, for example, Veena Das, Arthur Kleinman, Mamphele Ramphele, and Pamela Reynolds, eds. *Violence and Subjectivity* (Berkeley: University of California Press, 2000); Arthur Kleinman, Veena Das, and Margarat Lock, eds., *Social Suffering* (Berkeley: University of California Press, 1997); and Nancy Scheper-Hughes, *Death Without Weeping: The Violence of Everyday Life*

in Brazil (Berkeley: University of California Press, 1992).

13. Thomas J. Csordas, "Introduction: The body as representation and being-in-the-world," in *Embodiment and Experience*, 1–26.

14. Janelle S. Taylor, "On Recognition, Caring, and Dementia" *Medical Anthropology Quarterly*, 22:4 (Dec 2008): 313–335.

15. Lenore M. Buckley, *Talking with Patients about the Personal Impacts of Illness: The Doctor's Role* (Oxford: Radcliffe, 2008).

16. See M. Simone Roach, *The Human Act of Caring: A blueprint for the health professions* (Ottawa: Canadian Hospital Association, 1992).

17. Joan C. Tronto, *Moral Boundaries: A Political Argument for an Ethic of Care* (New York: Routledge, 1993).

18. For example, see William James, *The Varieties of Religious Experience: A Study in Human Nature* (New York: Random House, 1902).

19. Arthur Kleinman, *What Really Matters: Living a Moral Life Against Uncertainty and Danger* (Oxford: Oxford University Press, 2006).

The Life of Humans and the Life of Roaming Spirits

Veena Das [1]

In my work on violence and the everyday,[2] I have thought of the condition of human beings in their everyday existence as that of being not quite alive to themselves or as Stanley Cavell put it, "as not awake to their lives."[3] Pursuit of the moral then might be thought of as being called to awaken from forgetfulness. How does one awaken?

In this paper, I would like to evoke the complexity arising from being called to awaken by another. Lévinas' signature theme of the face as the emblem of the other along with his idea of the asymmetry of my relation to the other standing in an accusatory or persecutory relation to me, suggests some of this experience. From the infinite and the completely unknowable other to the concrete other in the figures of the widow, the orphan, and the stranger, Lévinas recognizes that a violence occurs in opening to the claims of the other. This violence comes from outside us, as Cavell notes in discussing Lévinas, "Lévinas' idea is that my openness to the other—to a region 'beyond' my narcissism—requires a violence associated with the infinite having been put into me. . . . This event creates as it were an outside to my existence, hence an isolated, singular inside."[4] From here Cavell reformulates the problem of responsibility to the other as originating not in the recognition of finitude in relation to the infinite nature of the other, but in the recognition that the particular other who is part of my existence is also completely separate from me. "The extravagant intimacy at stake in these relations [i.e. of Shakespearean characters such as Hamlet and his mother and Othello and his wife] suggests that the 'proof' of the other's existence is a problem not of establishing connection with the other, but of achieving or suffering, separation from the other, individuation with respect to the one upon whom my nature is staked."[5] Taking a cue from Cavell, then, the issue is not only the intuition of the infinite involved in this trauma, but rather the recognition that my responsibility to the other can only be a finite one—limiting the desire for infinite responsibility to the other is paradoxically what might attach one to life itself. It explains to me my own sense of the moral as a move, not towards the transcendental but towards an awakened everyday from the rote everyday: not an escape from the everyday but an embracing of it. Or to use one of Cavell's intellectual insights, it is the relation we establish between the actual everyday and the eventual everyday.[6]

How was *this* idea planted in me in my relation to my ethnographic sites? Scenes of visitations from the dead involve this question of responsibility to the concrete other, and thus also further the conversation between the finite limit of relations and the desire for the infinite. The urban neighborhoods in Delhi where I have worked for several years are composed of various kinds of beings—life is not simply the relations humans have with each other. According to many people from these neighborhoods with whom I have conversed, forms of gods and goddesses dwell there as well as ghosts, jinns, visions of people with light dripping from their faces (angels?), and of course the recently dead who can only be sensed through calling upon the inner senses. The commerce between such forms of life is not bound by caste or sect or language. The human body and the human senses receive these neighbors in an astonishing multiplicity of forms.

In this paper, I argue that the nonhuman functions in some lives to make them more wakeful, to recognize the specificity of their lives away from their abstract humanity or animality. In that sense we might best understand questions about human and nonhuman by looking at the relations of specific individual humans to specific individual nonhumans, for questions of "our humanity" are posed not in the abstract but in the rough and tumble of our actual lives.

My argument removes questions about human life from theories of virtue that consider morality as a form of rule following. In long periods of ethnographic work I have conducted in low-income neighborhoods in Delhi, spanning from the 1970s, I have listened to discussions of what one ought or ought not to do in general, but found that the most compelling moments arise when someone responds to events that put his or her entire life into question. Such moments often include the mediation of a nonhuman form of life into the rhythms of the everyday. A deity might come and possess someone, making them give expressions to desires they had never known to be theirs. At other times, beings that dwell in the world with humans, even in only a virtual existence—beings lost through death, or betrayal, or sheer forgetfulness of their existence—become present in ways that press upon humans to attend to relationships they think best forgotten.

In such a scene of forgetfulness, how is one drawn to an examination of one's life? To illustrate this, I would like to tell the story of Billu, a story that exemplifies a conjugation between man and spirit both intimate and strange. Everyday life in this case secretes a dimension of reality in which Billu finds himself suspended between the hold of the past and the demands of the present. What finally reattaches him to life is not a grand resolution of the problems he faced but his acknowledgement of a limit through the force of a spirit which teaches him that the problem of the other is not that of (or only that of) establishing connections but also of suffering separation. For Billu, as we shall soon see, this separateness was imbued with the color of failure, perhaps a bitter compromise with the fact of having to live this kind of life and not another.

This story unfolds in the streets of low-income neighborhoods and urban slums in Delhi, where clusters of shanties, half-built houses and other forms of dwelling nestle with bustling markets in which billboards announce various electronic goods—televisions, computers, music systems, tape recorders, along with traditional items such as saris, bangles, grocery items, and the ubiquitous posters of film stars. But most intriguing are the offers of new medical technologies. One billboard in Hindi announces the services of a small clinic, "Here you can get MRI, CAT scan, pregnancy test—you can also get relief from the misdeeds of evil spirits and from magical spells cast over you."[7] This juxtaposition illustrates how new medical technologies function in the lives of the poor—redefining the body as a machine that can be forever mended and augmented—yet also grafting these new hopes into an existing set of relations within which life is marked by scarcity, enormous struggle for survival, and the logics of triage that people perform every day as they decide which lives are to be enhanced and which ones to let go.

This calculus of survival against the backdrop of bio-exchanges is highlighted in the growing anthropological literature on bio-exchanges that is exposing the inequities and even the violence that accompany such exchanges. Both Nancy Scheper-Hughes and Margaret Lock, two of the most influential authors in the field of medical anthropology, have shown that the movement of organs from the poor to the rich creates new perils for the poor who are organ donors even as it enhances the life of the rich.[8] In an important contribution, Lawrence Cohen draws attention to the panic-producing language of moral outrage in many of the debates on organ exchange and offers a more nuanced concept of "bioavailability." Cohen hopes that the concept of bioavailability will help to bring forth the imaginaries of the body[9] as a resource for supplementing other bodies, thus allowing various new ethical formations to be generated. The concept is flexible enough to cover forcible extraction of organs and also the processes through which the poor might themselves participate in sale of organs (their own and that of their family members) as a form of ethical self-making.[10] Productive as these thoughts are, the ethnographic details in Cohen's analysis are somewhat sparse—the full geography of the relations brought about by the possibility of organ exchange is not developed. The recent work of Jacob Coleman on blood donation camps organized by two important religious sects is ethnographically rich and theoretically innovative, but his emphasis is on anonymous blood donations as a public gift and relationships created at a distance.[11] Through Billu's story, I hope to show instead what happens to close relationships once the possibility of a new technology is introduced and what this can tell us about the human as embedded within a specific form of life and its kinship with the nonhuman as machine and as spirits.

Billu, his brother, and his son

Billu lived with his wife and two-year-old son in a rented room in a low-income neighborhood, overcrowded and with poor facilities for water and sanitation. He worked as a part-time gardener for a nearby factory and also supplemented his income by doing domestic work in a middle-class family. Unlike other households similar to Billu's in which women supplement the family income by part-time work as housemaids or by making small items at home to sell to shops on a piece-rate basis, Billu's wife could not engage in any income-generating activities as she was sickly and often required attention for varied medical conditions. Over the years Billu had accumulated massive debts due to medical contingencies as well as his desire for new goods. He accumulated money at times, but he could never retain any savings. Growth of markets for goods in low-income localities that offer ready credit has meant that the poor are being reconstituted as consumers, and often lured into buying television sets, refrigerators, or other items on hire purchase—schemes that inevitably lead to serious indebtedness. Since it is hard for the poor to borrow from formal institutions, they end up either relying on ties of kinship or borrowing from informal credit markets at extremely high rates of interest. Billu too had fallen into the cycle of buying an attractive item with a down payment, getting into debt, paying high rates of interest, and ultimately forfeiting or selling off the item. This is not the place to give a full history of his financial transactions over a period of time. The general observations I offer, however, are drawn from a detailed record of financial transactions collected by the ISERDD (Institute of Socio-Economic Research on Development and Democracy) team from similar households over a three-year period.[12] Here I will offer one or two examples of the pattern of income and expenditure and the modalities of decision making in Billu's household.

Because Billu had worked with the same employers for more than ten years, he could mobilize them through appeals to their sympathy for his hardships. Sometimes they would give him outright loans of money without interest that he promised to return but never could; at other times he has received monetary help for tiding over a particular crisis. These were not his main sources of credit, but the help provided by his two employers was not negligible either. The pathways he followed had the character of contingency—he might be able to get some money from one or other of his superiors at his work place, or from the household in which he did part-time work, but there were never any guarantees. One could describe him as following the moves of a gambler, not infrequent in the economic circumstances of many residents of low-income neighborhoods. For example, four years ago, through regular savings in a bank that the head of the household in which he worked insisted he deposit every month under a small savings scheme, he had saved enough money to begin to pay off his debt. But instead, he bought a *jhuggi* (shanty) on the border of Delhi and Uttar Pradesh. Over one year he made gradual improvements—a tin roof and a door which his employer had discarded. He was planning to convert the *jhuggi* into a brick and cement dwelling, but then many jhuggis in that locality were declared illegal because the builder who had sold them apparently never had legal rights over the land. Billu had to move back to a rented one-room windowless dwelling after losing all his investment.[13] On other occasions the moment he accumulated a little money, someone from his village would fall ill, or he would have to contribute money towards a wedding or a funeral in the village. The combination of factors that allow people like Billu to survive, living from one emergency to another, are made up of a complex formation of employers' needs for trustworthy labor, especially domestic labor; ideas about charity *(dana)* that lead employers to dispense money that stands somewhere between debt and charity; and shadows of old patron-client relations that continue to operate even within the informal cash economy.

A crisis Billu faced a couple of years ago was probably the worst in his recent memory. His elder brother, Ramvilas, who worked as domestic servant in an affluent household, acting as cook, odd-jobs man, and cleaner for their bachelor son who had set up a separate establishment, fell ill with what initially looked like a viral fever. Ramvilas bought some analgesics from the local pharmacist and continued to work since his employer was not inclined to give him leave for what the employer deemed a minor seasonal fever. The fever turned out to be a hepatitis infection. Ramvilas' condition rapidly deteriorated. By the time his employer paid serious attention to the illness, Ramvilas' kidneys were affected. His employer was quite distraught over his condition. Through personal contacts Ramvilas' employer was able to get him admitted to a private hospital where a well-known transplant surgeon agreed to perform a transplant operation free of cost. This is less surprising than it seems since many private hospitals that have been given government land on subsidized rates must make provisions for treatment for a small percentage of their cases to be drawn from poor populations. Also in this case Billu's brother's employer was an influential businessman. However, other facilities were not free, and while Ramvilas awaited his turn for a kidney to become available, he had to be put on dialysis. His employer, having already spent a good amount of money on him, agreed to pay part of the costs but asked that the family contribute some part of the expenditure. Ramvilas had no one else to turn to, so Billu ended up borrowing more money from his own employers to meet this contingency. He showed them the various hospital records and even took his brother to their house so they could see for themselves what a pitiable condition Ramvilas was in. Some of Billu's neighbors tried to persuade him to send his brother to an *ashram* in the pilgrimage city of Rishikeh where he would be looked after, advising him that he might not be able to sustain the medical expenses over time. Billu's employers also tried to make him aware of the exorbitant costs of postoperative care and immune suppressant medicines and to urge him to think beyond the actual surgery.

But what weighed most heavily on Billu was his brother's heartbreaking pleas that he "wanted to live." "I could not turn away from my brother," Billu told me, "for, I thought—what happens later, one can only wait and see (lit. *ham ne socha baad ki baad mein dekhi jayegi*)." As it happened, Billu's brother died before a suitable kidney became available. I think it is possible that Billu was secretly relieved that he was found not to be a good match for a transplant; otherwise he might have had to donate a kidney. His brother's death also solved the problem of how to raise more money for postoperative medications even if the operation had been successful.

I have told this story in straightforward, linear terms to provide the plot of the story. However, Billu told me the story in small fragments, an episode here and an episode there as it unfolded over three months when I was visiting the field site daily and also as he sought me out. The plotlike structure is my construction. Another event and a different set of constellations appeared in the telling of this story, surfacing only toward the end of the episode in the telling, though they must have been present in Billu's consciousness throughout the time he was dealing with his brother's illness. This final burst of revelation, as I will describe later, seemed to suggest that the event of the brother's death was shot through with another experience of death for Billu, about which he was very reluctant to talk.

Another Event Casts its Shadow on Billu's Story

At first glance, this seems a simple story of kinship obligations and the normative force of kinship in the lives of the poor. However, not all his relatives exercised the same pull on Billu. Furthermore, while kinship is a source of solidarity and social support in many cases, kinship relations, especially between brothers, are often fraught with conflict.[14] So we would have to go beyond general appeals to kinship norms to understand Billu's desperate desire to help his brother. What was the texture of emotions that bound the two brothers? Billu had come to the city when he was quite young to work along with his brother. His father had died when he was barely five years old. With a small plot of land and six children to feed, his mother had found it difficult to provide for them. When Billu was only eleven or twelve years old, he came to the city and found employment as domestic help.

Billu told me that though his mother had sent him off with his brother and in a way abandoned him, she and his other siblings had often turned to him for his help once he started earning. It is hard for me to discern what he really felt for his mother—his characterizations of her were often contradictory. He felt she was taking advantage of him and yet she was his mother. He felt a son who abandoned his mother could find no happiness in this or any other life. Like many other migrants to the city, Billu would sometimes attempt to hide his money by keeping it as credit with his employers, but he often gave in to his mother's pleas for help. It was not simply that he considered it a moral obligation to help family back in the village, but that he also felt the attraction of being recognized as a dutiful son and a man of means back in the village. Yet, Billu also recognized that this effort drained him of any possibility of building a reasonably secure future for himself. His brother had been his biggest support in the city—the only close relative he had known throughout his childhood. He felt a special bond to him. When his brother died Billu felt the force of his own failure mixed with helplessness but also relief. This mixture of emotions animate the story: he could articulate how he had failed his brother but could never speak of how his brother's life might have drained him of his own life. A straightforward narrative in terms of plot and characters leaves out the force of that which remained mostly unsaid in his story and that which burst out on occasions without ever being integrated into the story he was ready to tell of his brother's death.

For all the love Billu had for his brother, there was one event that could enrage him whenever he talked about it, even after many years had passed. This was a marriage his mother had arranged for him in the village in which his brother had apparently connived. Lured by promises of a dowry, Billu's mother had arranged his marriage when he was barely fifteen to a much older woman. Soon after the marriage this woman ran away with another man alleging, falsely according to Billu, that he was "not a man."[15] Billu refused to return to the village, even for occasional visits, after that episode and for some years did not talk to his mother and brother. Subsequently, he arranged for his own marriage through a neighbor. The girl, his present wife, was older than him and turned out to be sickly, but he was determined to make a "good life" with her. The marriage cost him a fair amount of money since the bride's parents begged him to bear the expenses of the bridal meal and later refused to reimburse him for it. Nevertheless, against the usual aura of superiority that wife-takers maintain in Hindu marriages laying all problems in a marriage to the door of the wife, Billu could not bring himself to blame his wife. He repeatedly reiterated that it was not her fault that her parents were so cheap. "I have never eyed anyone's money," he told me. From my years in this and similar neighborhoods, I can vouch that this was not the usual rhetorical stance through which moral claims are made by everyone from local politicians to the shopkeepers who fleece those in need by the high rates of interest they charge. Instead his claim of caring for his wife and not for the material goods she came with was grounded in the small everyday acts through which he showed his love and care for her. I have seen him cook early morning before he goes off to work, fetch water from the municipal tap since water supply is irregular, and try his best to comfort his wife during her frequent episodes of illness.

Two years after their marriage a son was born to them, but he died within the first month. From Billu's descriptions of the symptoms I suspect it might have been a congenital heart condition which remained undiagnosed. Billu used the term he often uses to describe how he cared for someone by saying "*bahut seva kari, jitna ho saka seva kari par nahin baccha paya* (I served him a lot, as much as I was capable of serving him, but I could not save him)."

After this son's death Billu began to have visions and dreams in which a woman in white beckoned him to come to her. He was frightened of this woman but could not decipher what she wanted. After many consultations with the local *ojhas* (diviners), he understood that the woman in white was a form of the goddess of his home village *(gramdevata)* who blamed him for having forgotten the village. Billu arranged for a propitiation ceremony to placate the goddess, but in turn he set the condition that he would visit the village only after he was granted another son. The woman in white advised him to establish a silver idol of baby Krishna and also to make a pledge to perform *karseva* (acts of service such as sweeping the floors) at the local Gurudwara (Sikh temple) and especially to accept Guru Gobinda of the Sikh faith as his own guru. This complicated nexus of sacred beings across caste, sect, religion, and locality combined to create a singular sacred being with whom the devotee enters into an individualized relation is common for Hindus. In this case it draws from etymological connections—one of Krishna's names is Gobinda (cowherd) referring to his pastoral past. Connecting this with the Sikh guru on the basis of a common name participates in a form of reasoning prevalent in these neighborhoods in which similar names are made the basis of a mystical, hidden connection. (Sometimes children who have the same name will call each other *"sahnam"*—the one bearing the same name— rather than use their proper names.) So, at the behest of this goddess (whose identity remains obscure to Billu, despite the *ojha's* divination), he became a devotee of the child Krishna and a regular attendee in the local Sikh temple. He also pledged to call his child Gobinda.

Billu's efforts to placate and please the various figures mentioned here bore positive results, and a second child was born whom he duly named Gobinda after the baby Krishna and the Sikh guru. The silver idol of the Krishna figure had been established in the house, and Billu went with his wife and newborn child to the village to offer thanks. About two years after this event, Billu's brother fell sick and died leaving Billu sad but also guilt ridden that he had not been able to do enough for his brother.

Although Billu did not mention it while he related this story in bits and pieces whenever we met, it turned out that at this time his wife had become pregnant again. In the process of running around between hospitals, his work, the various local diviners, and various agencies from which he had tried to get charitable donations for his brother's treatment, Billu just could not find the time to attend to his wife. Unlike many other women in the area who are quite resourceful in accessing locally available medical care, Billu's wife, although born and bred in the city, had never been able to care for herself. At the last moment, Billu found a locally trained midwife to assist at the delivery, but the newborn son died of an infection the next day. Billu's brother died about one month before the birth, although Billu only brought up this son's death much later in casual conversation when I happened to ask him how his wife and children were doing. Since having moved to the U.S. I had not been able to visit him for many months after his brother's death.

Billu told me that after his brother's death he started having visions and dreams in which his brother would appear to him and accuse him of not caring for him. Billu always woke up frightened—the dreams were like coming face to face with an accusing figure he hardly knew, rather than the brother he had known and loved, however ambiguously. He became convinced that the newborn child had been a reincarnation of Ramvilas, his brother, but that in his anger Ramvilas had refused to make a life with Billu and to accept Billu's service *(seva)*. This explained why the brother/son had decided to die. I note the cultural resonance with the widely held idea that a newborn has to be persuaded to make life with the family he or she has been born into since the soul of the newborn is still attached to the life it left behind, as well as with the idea that the recently dead are so attached to the living that they will try to take one of them in their new journey.[16]

Specific to Billu's visions is the manner in which the possibilities of modernity fold into his life—new technologies such as transplant operations are both within sight of the poor now and yet often remain out of reach. These multiple possibilities create the singularity of the inner in which the responsibility for concrete others continually expands and can rarely be fulfilled. For Billu the matter was laid to some rest by the vision of the woman in white who appeared to him and admonished him for not accepting the conditions she had placed upon him. This is how he said she admonished him:

> "I told you that I would give you a son—that he would be blessed for he would carry the blessings of the baby Krishna and of Guru Gobinda. I did not tell you that you could now call upon me to deal with every misfortune.

Anything that takes you away from serving that son—my blessing, my *prasad* (offering made to a god or goddess and returned to the devotee with his or her blessing imbued in it) in your house—the son who is yours only so long as it pleases me—anything that turns you away from him will incur my anger. I took responsibility only for him—not for anyone else—go and serve him."

Billu said he felt truly frightened of her, but perhaps she gave him some peace too. He repeatedly said that he could not understand the woman/goddess in white. If she is a goddess, is she asking me not to pay attention to the needs of my mother who gave me life or my brothers who are my blood? She is the one who sent me back to the village, but is it now her desire that I serve her only through the medium of my son?

Billu's relation to this spirit hangs suspended between trust and suspicion. Here is where his sense of failure that I hinted at in the opening pages of this essay becomes most acute. Billu's ambivalence towards concentrating on his everyday life, separating from the needs of more distant others (his mother, his brother, his village), is marked by a complex network of feelings of relief, failure, and compromise. He has suffered not only the separateness from the other, but also an implicit indictment of himself. Billu's story exemplifies the limits of both rational argumentation as well as the impossibility of staging emotion as reason's counterpart. He conveys the events of life not as a linear narrative, but as a series of more and less wakeful moments.

Questions and Reflections

What is the pressure on thought that a case such as this might put on us? In thinking about Billu's story and its implications for understanding the human, I turn to the philosopher Stephen Mulhall, writing on the theme of the human and humanity:

> . . . our concept of a person is an outgrowth or aspect of our concept of a human being; and that concept is not merely biological but rather a crystallization of everything we have made of our distinctive species nature. To see another as a human being is to see her as a fellow creature—another being whose embodiment embeds her in our distinctive form of common life. . . .
>
> . . . nonhuman animals too, can be seen as our fellow

creatures in a different but related sense of the term. Their embodied existence, and hence their form of life is different; but in certain cases the human and the nonhuman form of creaturely existence can overlap, interact, even offer companionship to one another, and in many cases nonhuman animals can be seen as sharing a common fate with us.[17]

For Mulhall, we can see our connectedness to the nonhuman forms of life because of our embodiment: we share with animals the facts of a creaturely existence—susceptibility to pain, disease, and death. Embodiment, however, is no guarantee of understanding. In Wittgenstein's famous formulation, if a lion could speak how would we understand what he had to say?[18] We share our vulnerability to death and disease with animals, but another vulnerability sets us apart from animals—our vulnerability to language. What if certain forms of nonhuman life that we imagine are embodied differently from humans and the language such beings use to express themselves partakes of our language but is also strange to it? Anthropologists have often imagined[19] that our kinship with animals expresses our kinship with gods and spirits, unlike the metaphysical imagination of Descartes in which our turning to the divine is a *turning away* from our animal nature and relegating the body to being mere machine.

Billu's story suggests that the inhuman or nonhuman might teach us ways of being human in a spirit of wakefulness to ourselves and to others. Mulhall's quotation comes from his consideration of J.M. Coetzee's literary figure, Mrs. Costello, and the issues raised there on the condition of humans and of animals. In Coetzee's *The Lives of Animals* and *Elizabeth Costello*,[20] the main character, Elizabeth Costello, is a novelist and animal rights activist who mainly appears to us through a series of lectures and the events surrounding them. She suffers and expresses that suffering. Response to Coetzee's work has produced a stunning set of literary and philosophical reflections on how human beings wound each other in the course of their daily living.[21] These deliberations compel us to ask how our companionship with each other and with nonhuman forms of life might be acknowledged despite or along with this wounding. The dominant sense on reading these musings by some of philosophy's most accomplished writers remains what Cora Diamond calls the "difficulty of reality."[22] There is something resistant to thought when we try to imagine the condition of being wounded that Mrs. Costello experiences when she sees ordinary and apparently nice people indifferently consuming animals killed for food. Something other than rational argumentation is called for in the face of this condition, not simply emotion or empathy as opposed to reason, but wakefulness—the state Billu reaches after the woman in white speaks to him about his duty to his son and the state in which we hope to listen to his story.

Cavell might say that Billu experienced finite responsibility—the spirit's command to care only for his son—as further wounding that forced him to reside in the ambiguities of wakefulness after the initial wounding of caring for others such as his brother. The events that cause his life to become a question to him include human and nonhuman forces, both the potentiality of organ transplant and the commands of the lady in white. Through her, we recognize that the desires that move beings such as gods, goddesses, ancestors, or jinns implicate human beings in their fulfillment but also pose great risks for the humans involved. Some concerns about the desires of the spirits map to specific traditions that Hindus or Muslims evoke within Hinduism or Islam, but frequently divine desire crosses both social boundaries and boundaries between life and death. In his visions, Billu was confronted with two different modalities in which the occult world made its presence felt in the world of the living. In one modality, the dead seem to have entailments in the actual world—they had a history that connected them with the living in which love, betrayal, failed promises, and unrealized hopes provide some guidance to the living on how to interpret the sightings or hearings with which the living are confronted. Error and doubt are as much a part of this experience as belief, a reminder of the vulnerability to which human action is subject—mistakes made, excuses offered, guilt for failures in relationship. Such interpretations have most often been brought to mind when a dead relative returned. Although in Billu's case he was the one who stood accused, in other cases the dead themselves seek forgiveness. For instance, a father who had been unable to marry off his daughter because he had been too proud to accept any of the offers that came for her hand would appear in her dreams to seek her forgiveness so that he could be released from the sin of failing to perform the most sacred duty a Hindu father is expected to perform for a daughter. In either case there is a history to the relationship in which the possible world in which the dead now live carries with it memories of the world in which actions were undertaken, often unsuccessfully—a past imperfect that continues to impinge upon the possible world in which the dead are imagined to be now having a life.

The modality of the lady in white was different. Her initial actions in insisting that Billu return to the village to placate the local goddess revealed her to be that local goddess but displaced from the village. At one level then she created conditions for the continuity of Billu's relation to the village. Yet as events developed in Billu's life, she insisted that Billu limit his sense of infinite responsibility to the relations that were devouring him and commit himself to ensuring the survival of the child that he had received as her blessing. A simple explanation might be that her appearance authorized him to separate himself from the terrible responsibilities for the village that he was unable to meet and that this vision was a rationalization of his desire to dissociate himself from his past. There is surely some element of truth in such an explanation. However, the goddess in white belonged to a class of beings who could not be fully assimilated with gods, goddesses, or spirits whose mythologies, forms of rituals, or character were fully known. In this sense these emergent beings were like the emergent technologies whose form was transfigured as they were detached from the places in which they properly belong. Yet these two emergent entities took different lines of flight. The technologies expanded hope invested in the idea of the body as a machine while expanding the scope of obligations to kin to such an extent that the immediacy of material conditions and their limitations disappear from view. Conversely the goddess in white attached Billu to his immediate life asking him to saturate his immediate surroundings with care and love and make it livable. Two forms of inhuman then conjugate with the human, one drawing the human figure toward kinship with machines and the second toward a relationship with beings of the occult world. The person then is an aspect of this conjugation of human and inhuman rather than an aspect of humanity as an abstract concept.

These relationships also draw attention to the capacity of human beings for displacement. While well-defined ritual procedures might be described in terms of the felicity conditions for illocutionary acts enumerated by Austin[23] (especially the importance of first-person-singular utterances such as "I promise" or "I declare" and the stability of context), the visions and dreams that Billu and many others described to me might be thought of as improvisations on traditionally stable ritual acts in which the *addressee* is singled out and known as the recipient of the command/desire of the being that has chosen to speak, but the being itself has no clear standing. Billu did not recognize the lady in white—initially she established her position by making him see what he had ignored, his obligation to the village. Then she freed him from that very same obligation, the past which was taking away his capacity to live in the present. Meanwhile she also managed to establish herself as a goddess to be worshipped. Benjamin famously distinguished between mythic violence and divine violence and saw the former as establishing the subject as one bound to the law while the latter struck against the injustice of law itself.[24] While many criticize Benjamin for not distinguishing sufficiently between law itself and the injustices of certain laws,[25] Benjamin's insight forces our attention to the idea that law as rule following might drain us of life, in the sense that our life might become machinelike. One reading of the bitter compromise or the difficulty of reality that we see in Billu's life is that, in his return to the everyday, he acknowledged the limits of his flesh-and-blood human self.

NOTES

1. I am grateful to the participants in the seminar on the theme of "Rethinking the Human," held at the Center for the Study of World Religions for their comments. I thank the editors for their encouragement on developing this paper and especially Susan Lloyd McGarry for the work she put in to amplify and clarify the main argument. To the person I call Billu, his family, and the household in which he worked and to whom he introduced me, I am grateful for discussions on how to raise resources for such contingencies as he faced. Almost all the interviews took place within that frame of discussion as I also helped Billu to write applications, find addresses, and put him in contact with other patients awaiting kidney transplants so that he could learn what this surgery entailed. I continued to run into him whenever I visited his neighborhood so that the conversations continued over one year. Ethnographic work itself has its moments when reality seems quite unbearable.

My general understanding of urban transformations in the neighborhoods in Delhi owes much to the work of members of Institute of Socio-Economic Research on Development and Democracy (ISERDD), a research and advocacy organization in Delhi of which I am a founding member and with whom I have worked closely in building longitudinal data on a panel of 400 households since 2000. Though Billu is not part of that panel of households, his story resonates with that of others in the neighborhoods on which systematic information has been compiled by ISERDD members. I thank Charu, Harpreet Geeta, Purhottam, Poonam, and Rajan for many discussions on urban poverty and their dedication to the ongoing work on urban and rural poverty. I am indebted to Paola Marratti for discussions on issues of the human and the inhuman in the course of a joint course we taught. To Ranen and Jishnu my thanks for their generous intellectual and practical support.

2. See most recently Veena Das, *Life and Words: Violence and the Descent into the Ordinary* (Berkeley: University of California Press, 2007).

3. Stanley Cavell, *Philosophy the Day after Tomorrow* (Cambridge: Belknap Press of Harvard University Press, 2005), 214.

4. Ibid., 145. In the essay in this book, "The Scandal of Skepticism," Cavell discusses Lévinas and these ideas. For more specifically from Lévinas himself, see Emmanuel Lévinas, *The Lévinas Reader*, ed. Seán Hand (Malden, MA: Blackwell Publishers, 1989) provides a good introduction. For more on the face and the other, see 82–85, for example.

5. Cavell, *Philosophy The Day After*, 146.

6. This theme is especially poignant in Stanley Cavell's understanding of America as a country that has not found its voice, philosophically speaking. This idea is found in several of Cavell's books including *This New Yet Unapproachable America* (Albuquerque, NM: Living Batch Press, 1989). Among his many commentators, Simon Critchley and Sandra Laugier are especially attentive to this strand of Cavell's thought. Critchley writes about the attempt to recover the American romantic tradition and the sadness of "an unworked America

that hesitates in the tension between nihilism and its overcoming, between the actual everyday and the eventual everyday." See Simon Critchley, "Cavell's 'Romanticism' and Cavell's Romanticism," in *Contending with Stanley Cavell,* ed. Russell B. Goodman (New York: Oxford University Press, 2005), 47. See also Sandra Laugier, "Rethinking the Ordinary" in the same book, 82–99.

7. See Veena Das and Ranandra K. Das, "How the Body Speaks" in *Subjectivity: Ethnographic Explorations,* ed. Joao Biehl, Byron Good, and Arthur Kleinman (Berkeley: University of California Press, 2007).

8. See for example Nancy Scheper-Hughes, "Rotten Trade: Millennial Capitalism, Human Values and Global Justice in Organs Trafficking," in *Human Rights: an Anthropological Reader,* ed. Mark Goodale (Malden, MA: Wiley-Blackwell, 2009), 167–197, and Margaret M. Lock, Allan Young, Alberto Cambrosio et al., *Living and Working with the New Medical Technologies: Intersections of Inquiry* (Cambridge: Cambridge University Press, 2000).

9. By imaginaries of the body I mean that even when practices through which the body is located in the social world do not change, what one imagines can be done with the body changes.

10. See Lawrence Cohen, "Operability, Bioavailability, and Exception," in *Global Assemblages: Technology, Politics, and Ethics as Anthropological Problems,* ed. Aihwa Ong and Stephen J. Collier (Malden, MA: Blackwell Publishing, 2005), 79–90.

11. See Jacob Coleman, *Veins of Devotion: Blood Donation and Religious Experience in North India* (New Brunswick: Rutgers University Press, 2009).

12. The ISERDD team collects information on main events in a household by visiting the sample households in each neighborhood at least once in three months. These events include any major financial transaction, such as the sale or purchase of assets, debts taken, credit given as well as other events in the household such as births, marriages and deaths. Though these data have not yet been fully analyzed, I can attest to the fact that the financial transactions that the poor enter into are extremely complex. I kept information that Billu offered in a diary for over one year—though it is notoriously difficult to find accurate data on all financial transactions since people often remember only the big events, my sense is that the general description that Billu related about his financial situation and the strategies he used for both survival and for maintaining relationships was not unique. Strong support for the complexity of the financial transactions of poor households is provided by the excellent analysis of financial diaries kept by a small sample of poor households in three countries (India, Bangladesh and South Africa) contained in the path-breaking book, *Portfolios of the Poor: How the World's Poor Live on $2 a Day* by Daryl Collins, Jonathan Morduch, Stuart Rutherford, and Orlanda Ruthven (Princeton: Princeton University Press, 2009).

13. The question of how one acquires rights over a dwelling is extremely complex. Conflicting laws and court judgments sometimes allow people below a certain level of poverty to retain rights over small plots of land even if these were

illegally occupied: the courts have argued that the constitutional right to life binds the State to provide housing to the poor and that someone who can show continuous dwelling in one place cannot be displaced without being given alternate provisions. However, since Billu had "bought" the shanty in which he lived rather than simply "occupied" it, he could not make claims for ownership over his dwelling once the seller was shown to have no rights over that plot of land. For an excellent discussion of the fragmentation of legal practices, formal and informal, as well as the constellation of state and nonstate actors in these practices, see Julia Eckert, "Urban Governance and Emergent Forms of Legal Pluralisms in Mumbai," *Journal of Legal Pluralism*, 2004 (50): 29–60.

14. See Veena Das, "Masks and Faces: An Essay on Punjabi Kinship," *Contributions to Indian Sociology*, (n.s.) 1976 (1): 1–30.

15. This part of the story is reconstructed from conversations I had with his wife on earlier occasions in varied contexts—especially when she was fed up with the money that Billu felt compelled to spend on his mother.

16. On the idea that the dead have to be persuaded to leave the living and move on to their own worlds, see Jean M Langford, "Spirits of Dissent: Southeast Asian Memories and Disciplines of Death" in *Comparative Studies of South Asia, Africa and the Middle East*, 2005, Vol. 25 (1): 161-176. On the newborn's attachment to his or her previous life, see Das, "Masks and Faces."

17. Stephen Mulhall, *The Wounded Animal: J.M. Coetzee and the Difficulty of Reality* (Princeton: Princeton University Press, 2009), 31, 32.

18. Many writers about Wittgenstein refer to this lion. See, for example, Simon Glendinning, *On Being With Others* (New York: Routledge, 1998), 71 or Brian McGuiness, *Approaches to Wittgenstein, Collected Papers* (New York: Routledge, 2002), the first chapter is called "The lion speaks, and we don't understand," 3–7.

19. The classic position on this might be said to be that of Émile Durkheim, *The Elementary Forms of Religious Life*, transl. Carol Cosman, ed. Mark S. Cladis (London: Oxford University Press, 2001) originally published in French in 1912.

20. J.M. Coetzee, *The Lives of Animals*, ed. Amy Guttman (Princeton: Princeton University Press, 2001); and J.M. Coetzee, *Elizabeth Costello* (New York: Viking Books, 2003).

21. Stanley Cavell, Cora Diamond, John McDowell et al, *Philosophy and Animal Life* (New York: Columbia University Press, 2008).

22. Cora Diamond, "The Difficulty of Reality and the Difficulty of Philosophy" in Cavell et al, *Philosophy and Animal Life*, 43–89.

23. J. L. Austin, *How to do Things with Words*, ed. J.O. Urmson and Marina Sbisà (Cambridge: Harvard University Press, 1962, second edition 1975) summarized on 53. Cavell has an interesting critique of the lack of consideration of passion in Austin's schema (and also cites the conditions that would make utterances with perlocutionary force felicitous thus allowing an expression of passion to be analyzed in the same way that conventional action is analyzed through the category of illocutionary force): see Cavell, *Philosophy the Day after*, 155–191.

24. Walter Benjamin, "Critique of Violence" in his *Reflections: Essays, Aphorisms, Autobiographical Writings*, ed. Peter Demetz (New York: Schoken Books, 1986), 277–300.
25. See for instance, Patricia Tuitt, "Individual Violence and the Law," *Studies in Law, Politics and Society* (ed. Austin Sarat) 2006, Vol. 39: 3–15.

The Secret of a Woman of Ninety: Rethinking the Very Long Life

For Nell Hallisey

Charles Hallisey[1]

The title of this essay contains an allusion and a reference; each provides a key orientation for this essay on how rethinking the very long life can help us to rethink the human. The allusion is to an idea in an essay by the early twentieth-century French essayist, Charles Péguy, in which he reflects on the significance of considering time when trying to understand the human by using a rubric of what he calls the secret of a man of forty.[2] The practice of writing history was of primary concern for Péguy in this essay and he used the idea of the secret of the man of forty—which he said all people learn in the course of reaching middle age—to argue that we should reconsider the aims of history writing and our approaches to it. It is Clio, the muse of history, who reveals the secret of the man of forty in Péguy's essay as she talks to Péguy about himself:

> Look, she said, at this man at forty. Maybe we know him, Péguy, our man of forty. Maybe we are beginning to know him. He is forty, so he *knows*. The knowledge that no teaching can impart, the secret that no method can prematurely entrust, the knowledge that no discipline confers nor is able to confer, the teaching that no school can disseminate, he *knows*. Being forty, he has, in the most natural way in the world, to say the least, received news of the secret that is known by most people in the world that is nonetheless the most hermetically kept.

For he knows the great secret of every creature, the secret that is most universally known but which, nonetheless, has never been leaked, . . . the secret that is the most universally entrusted, little by little, from one person to another, in a lowered voice, in the course of intimate conversations, in the privacy of confessions, on chance roadways, and yet the secret that is most hermetically secret . . .

He knows that *one* is not happy. He knows that ever since there has been man no man has ever been happy.[3] [Italics in original]

Clio then goes on, however, to point out another aspect of this man of forty:

Now, note the inconsistency. The same man. This man naturally has a son of fourteen. And he has but one thought, that his son should be happy. And he does not tell himself that it would be the first time, that this has yet to be seen. He tells himself nothing at all, which is the sign of the deepest thought. . . . He has an animal thought. Those are the best kind. . . . He thinks only of this, that his son should be happy. . . . That which has never succeeded, never happened, he is convinced will happen this time. And not only that, but that it will happen as if naturally and smoothly. As a result of some sort of natural law. And history said, I say that nothing is as touching as this perpetual, this eternal, this eternally reborn inconsistency; and that nothing is as disarming before God.[4]

For Péguy, becoming aware of "this perpetual, this eternal, this eternally reborn inconsistency" gives an occasion to ask essential questions about what we should expect of ourselves when we try to describe the aspirations and actions of others. What does it mean to write history when we know this secret and this inconsistency? How do we acknowledge in our reflections and writing, as Annette Aronowicz says of Péguy's approach, a "certain solidarity with those one is investigating, based not on party affiliation, religion, nationality, race, or gender, but on a common defeat in time and yet a sort of triumph within that defeat"?[5] What is the image of the human being that slowly comes into view from this "certain solidarity"?

In a similar vein to that traced by Péguy, I want to ask whether there is yet a further secret of common knowledge that our existence in time affords us, particularly whether there is a secret which the very long life makes us receptive to and another "sort of triumph" within the all-too-obvious defeats that come with the very long life. I have in mind a particular possibility of secret triumph as the secret of a woman of ninety.

There is, however, an important difference between my voice in this essay and Péguy's voice in his essay. The "Péguy" of the essay, the man of forty, knows that he knows the secret. I am neither a woman nor am I ninety; while I can grant the possibility of my becoming ninety, I do not grant the possibility of my becoming a woman of ninety. How then should I reflect on the significance of that secret for our task of rethinking the human when I can only anticipate the secret, imagine it, while admitting a considerable amount of distortion? This is an issue that can neither be avoided nor overcome. The threat of distortion is significant, but I believe that we must take on that risk, because to leave out the image of the human revealed in the very long life would be to seriously distort other images of the human that we might bring into sight for consideration and reflection.

As I consider this necessary distortion, the referent in my title becomes particularly important. I know the woman of ninety to which my title refers. She is my mother. As in Péguy's essay, where the importance of the particularity of the man of forty was acknowledged through the use of Péguy's name, so it is important to acknowledge the particularity of the woman of ninety in this essay. Her name is Nell Hallisey and she had just turned ninety a few weeks before I first presented this paper at the conference on "Rethinking the Human" at the Center for the Study of World Religions.

What I have to say about the secret of the woman of ninety in connection with my mother is personal, but I feel that it is not overly sentimental to turn to what I imagine and maybe even know of my mother's existential situation in this essay. Following Péguy in this, my mother has a secret that is forever "being divulged—in conversations, on chance roadways—[but] it remains secret"[6] from those like me, still only capable of having no more than faint inklings of it. At the heart of this essay is my knowledge that my mother has a secret now that she is in her nineties, and even though she may be divulging it to me "in conversations, on chance roadways," I know that I am not quite hearing it, because it is "hermetically kept" from me and "no school can impart it" just as the secret of the man of forty was kept from me earlier.

If I took as my concern in this essay "the secret of a man of ninety," it might be easier. I am a man. The epistemological condition constituted by an awareness of difference and not-knowing is qualitatively distinct from the epistemological condition relevant to ascertaining even an inkling of the secret of a woman of ninety. Again, it is a question of particularity. Already this particularity constitutes part of the image of the human towards which we are groping. Our individual capacity to know things about particular others, about individuals who are different from us also displays something important about ourselves.

Gender obviously does matter in how we age, but if we were to focus on how gender matters in aging, it would probably divert our attention away from the particular to the abstract, and away from a particular person to the shared structures and conditions of culture and society. The category of gender if employed too crudely may make it harder to discern even inklings of the secret of the woman of ninety.

The particularities of a very long life compel us to consider whether efforts to discern the secret of a woman of ninety might be better furthered not by a concern with gender and aging but rather by attention to gender and old age. The twentieth-century European philosopher Theodor Adorno can help us with this latter notion of old age, as different from a generic notion of aging. Adorno thought deeply about what it means to be extremely old and he tried to incorporate it into his own thinking about the human as he tried to make sense of the significance of old age itself as a human possibility. Indeed, it is in the midst of one of Adorno's reflections on old age that I found a powerful rationale for me to speak about my mother in this essay on rethinking the very long life and how this can help us to rethink what is the human.

Adorno, that most abstract of philosophers, reminds us that in encountering the particular we sometimes get a glimpse of the possibility of singularity in the human. He challenges us to consider how to make sense of this possibility of singularity as we rethink the general category of the human. Adorno, in one of his later lectures in his *Metaphysics*, which he delivered toward the end of his life, remarked:

> I am not speaking here of the discomforts associated with old age in the epic ideal. As far as my experience extends, there is also something immeasurably sad in the fact that with the decline of very old people the hope

> of *non confundar*,[7] of something which will be preserved
> from death, is also eroded, because, especially if one
> loves them, one becomes so aware of the decrepitude of
> that part of them which one would like to regard as the
> immortal . . . .[8]

Adorno's clause, "especially if one loves them," reminds us that the manner in which we relate to the people we love enhances and even extends what we are capable of seeing as we grope towards an image of the human. Adorno reminds us that we want to reflect on how we see other human beings with this clause in mind. Obviously it is an intimate engagement but I also think that it is analogous to "the certain solidarity with those one is investigating" that Péguy insisted on as a condition for historical knowledge. In the angle of vision that Adorno's phrase, "especially if one loves them," signals, we might also see something analogous to Péguy's "eternal, this eternally reborn inconsistency."

Changes in health care, public health, and in the economy over the last century have changed life expectancy and expanded the norms of human longevity. We know this. However, our ideas about aging and the aged have not changed in any degree close to the changes in the circumstances of the physical conditions of aging in our time, as Helen Small points out in her excellent book, *The Long Life*.[9] Some of our most common ideas about aging we can see already in Cicero in the first century BCE. For example, Cicero says our power to act nobly and our right to authority increase rather than diminish with age, because great deeds are the products of thought and character and judgment—all of which grow stronger with experience. He also says that there is nothing to fear about aging or being old, but instead it is an opportunity.[10] In such statements, we may feel an underlying unease with whether being aged is qualitatively different from earlier periods of life. Montaigne, commenting on Cicero, said he gives one an appetite for growing old, and we still have such ideas in our culture, particularly when we use them in the new idioms in which we speak about aging, such as "sixty is the new forty."[11]

Of course, there is another side. Our contemporary cultures also inherit a range of equally ancient ideas such as those expressed by the Buddha when he spoke about the First Noble Truth, "all this is suffering." When the Buddha began to substantiate what "all this" might be, right away he named old age, "old age is suffering."[12] So we have optimistic points of view from people like Cicero, but we also inherit pessimistic points of view from people like the Buddha. What is worth emphasizing here is that we still experience what being aged means today through such inherited ideas, even as the conditions of being humans who live to old age have changed—not only through increased life expectancy but through increased quality of life from better health care, better public health practices, and greater security from violence. These conditions for living longer and better are, of course, not found equally everywhere around the world. For example, life expectancy in Zimbabwe has gone down dramatically over the last decades because of a number of reasons, including social violence.[13] Unhappily, Zimbabwe is not a unique place in our world today.[14] The general point still holds: even with so many changes in the ways that we age and live, our experiences of aging and what is entailed in being old may have a greater consistency with the past than might be expected.

No matter how we perceive what it is like to be old, we also know that we experience the experience of aging in different ways over the course of our lifetimes. These differences are depicted in fiction. (As an aside, it is worth noting that fiction allows us to imagine what it is like to be very old without yet having reached old age, and what we come to know because of what we imagine through reading fiction can become part of the histories of our hearts.) In novels, we can listen to characters talk about the experience of aging and recognize what they are talking about. This is certainly true for myself. Sometimes characters in fiction speak about experiences that I myself have had and they ring true to me. For example, in Yukio Mishima's four-volume work, *The Sea of Fertility*, one of the characters, Shigekuni Honda, lives through all four volumes while the other protagonist is reincarnated in each of them. We thus see one man getting older and the other always staying young. We also see them interacting with each other through and against the historical backdrop of a particularly vivid time period in the history of modern Japan, from that of the Meiji period through the Second World War. In the second volume, *Runaway Horses*, Honda is thirty-eight years old. I myself read *The Sea of Fertility* when I was about eighteen and then by chance reread it when I was thirty-eight. When I was rereading the whole sequence of novels at age thirty-eight and turned to the beginning of the second volume, the comment about how "oddly situated a man is apt to find himself at age thirty-eight" made an impression on me that it had not when I read it twenty years earlier. Mishima continues,

> His youth belongs to the distant past. Yet the period of
> memory beginning with the end of youth and extending

to the present has left him not a single vivid impression. And therefore he persists in feeling that nothing more than a fragile barrier separates him from his youth. He is forever hearing with the utmost clarity the sounds of this neighboring domain, but there is no way to penetrate the barrier.[15]

A similar recognition happened to me recently when reading Richard Ford's novel, *The Lay of the Land*, in which the protagonist, Frank Bascombe, is in his fifties, (as I am now). Bascombe invokes a category, "the permanent period," which I have found so compelling that I have had recourse to it frequently since then. "The permanent period" is the way that Bascombe names the change in our idea and experience of the future as we age:

What it portended—and this is the truest signature of the permanent period—which comes by the way when it comes and not at any signifying age and not as a climacteric: not when you expect it, not when your ducks are in a row. . . —it portended an end to perpetual becoming, to thinking that life schemed wonderful changes for me, even if it didn't. It portended a blunt break with the past and provided a license to think of the past only indistinctly. . . . It portended that younger citizens might come up to me in wonderment and say, "How in the world do you live?" . . . It portended that I say to myself and mean it, even though I said it every day and already really meant it: "This is how in the shit I *am*! My life is *this* way"—recognizing, as I did, what an embarrassment and a disaster it would be if, once you were dust, the world and yourself were in basic disagreement on this subject.[16]

What Mishima is describing with Honda at age thirty-eight and Ford is describing with Bascombe in his fifties are men whose thinking about both the past and the future in their lives has changed radically as they age. What is important for our concerns in this essay is that these fictional characters remind us that the experience of aging itself changes as we age. The experience of aging for those already old may be categorically and qualitatively different than for those who are younger.

What might this experience of aging—and the world—by the old be like? Adorno introduced one possibility in his notion of "late style." As is well known, Adorno created this category while reflecting on the difference between symphonies Beethoven composed when young and his last symphonies. In the earlier ones the beauty comes from the harmonies and the patterns created, while the late symphonies seem discordant and disharmonized. Adorno explored the idea that this seeming discord expresses the experience of the later period in life, hence late style. As with Ford, chronological age may not dictate when this late style emerges. Late style can happen at different times of life, as can an appreciation of the worldview expressed in a late style. Adorno was in his twenties when writing about Beethoven's late style. Edward Said, who explored, extended, and popularized Adorno's ideas about late style, did so towards the end of his own life. In fact, Said's book, *On Late Style*, was published posthumously. Said's elaborations of Adorno associated the emergence of a late style with awareness of an end to life, something commonly associated with old age. Finding that things in the world do not fit together into an obvious whole, accepting that things are contingent, finding that things in the world are discordant, but still finding beauty there without trying to craft all together into a simpler picture—these are features of a late style.[17]

Returning to Péguy's question, how do we write history—which is really nothing more than writing about other people in different times and places—with the possibility of a late style in mind? We can glimpse the benefits of doing so if we consider Shinran and Dogen, major Buddhist thinkers from medieval Japan. We tend to think of Shinran and Dogen as two great Japanese thinkers from the twelfth century, seeing commonality in them as cultural products of the same time period. However, when we look at their lives, we immediately see that they are quite different in terms of how long each lived. Shinran lived until he was ninety, Dogen died when he was fifty.[18] When we read their writings, should we not keep in mind the difference in their ages when they wrote? Some of Shinran's greatest writings were works of his seventies. Some of his most distinctive ideas he returned to when he was close to ninety. Moreover, Shinran's greatest work, *Kyogyoshinsho*, "True Teachings on the Pure Land Way,"[19] epitomizes late style: he brings together passages from authoritative Buddhist texts in ways in which it is frequently hard for us to understand his larger point. Shinran must have intended to convey certain meanings because he sometimes changed the wording of quotations from Buddhist scriptures; when the words in the received scriptures did not say what he wanted them to say, he gave himself the license to change the text on the basis of his own experience and did not try to harmonize the quotations by these changes either. The passages collected together in Kyogyoshinsho do not form an obvious whole.

Shinran's later writings, including one of the last letters that Shinran wrote at age eighty-six, return to one of his most central ideas, *jinen*. *Jinen* can be translated as "made to become so." Shinran takes this idea of "made to become so" as a nuanced account of salvation. For Shinran, to be saved by the workings of Amida Buddha's Vow[20] is to become aware that one was made to become saved. Exactly what is happening here? What was Shinran seeing when he said that the key to the possibility of what is most good in our life is *jinen*, that we were "made to become so?" He said this when he was in old age; in the midst of personal tragedies, including having to disown the son he had chosen as his successor in the movement that he founded, and in the midst of the tolls that we can imagine old age was taking on his body—in the middle of all this he said that we were made to become so and this is our salvation.[21]

We can look at other resources, as well as general patterns of Buddhist soteriology, when trying to understand what Shinran meant by "we are made to become so" in a specifically Buddhist sense. At the same time, Shinran's words seem quite similar to those of Simone de Beauvoir describing what it means to become old. This may help us to see that Shinran is speaking of something that is more than just "Buddhist." De Beauvoir says that as we grow old:

> We must assume a reality that is certainly ourselves, although it reaches us from the outside and although we cannot grasp it. There is an insoluble contradiction between the obvious clarity of the inward feeling that guarantees our unchanging quality and the objective quality of our transformation. All we can do is waver from one to the other, never managing to hold them both firmly together.[22]

De Beauvoir's observations seem quite close to Shinran's on *jinen*. *Jinen*, "made to become so," is a reality that is "certainly ourselves," although it seems to reach us from the outside and we cannot grasp it, just as de Beauvoir says happens with aging. Shinran sees an insoluble contradiction between the obvious clarity of the inward feeling that guarantees our unchanging quality—in Shinran's case, it is that "I am a foolish being mired in evil"—and the objective certainty of our transformation by the workings of Amida Buddha's Vow to save us. In both Shinran and de

Beauvoir, we waver from one to the other, never managing to hold them firmly together in experience, even though both coinhere in our lives. "Never managing to hold them both firmly together" is a good account of late style.

We have to ask whether "extreme old age" is something again quite different from merely being old? Medicine acknowledges this by dedicating a field to the study and treatment of extremely old people, senescence (rather than only gerontology, the study of aging and old people). Those who have lived very long lives are not just experientially and socially different from those who are younger, they are also physically different. My mother called me up with happiness some time ago to tell me that she is now too old to get Alzheimer's—it was something that she had recently heard in a news report. News reports on science are not always reliable, but mortality rates do seem to change in the very old in surprising ways, as can be seen in actuarial tables. Once people get to a certain age, the percentage of those who pass away increases at a much slower rate. It almost seems to plateau.[23] The risk of death for the very old thus is different than people who may seem close to them in age—after all, they both are in the category of "old"—but the very old are living in a different physical condition. This change in mortality rates resonates with de Beauvoir's observation that old age is "a reality that is certainly ourselves" but is "from the outside."

Trying to understand what is happening to the bodies of the very old has generated new fields of medicine, with certainly unfamiliar and often unpronounceable names like pleiotropy (although this field of genetics does investigate patterns of physical development in the full range of human bodies). Other areas of medicine resort to metaphors to describe aging bodies, for example, comparing the body in old age to a genetic dustbin. There are suggestions that substances suppressed earlier in our bodies now can no longer be suppressed and may now take an even greater toll on us because of that suppression. My point here is less a scientific one than a phenomenological one. Our bodies at a biological and genetic level seem to be a reality that is us but is also outside us and can do to us what we do not want. This raises difficult questions, both theoretically and practically. How do we understand ourselves? Would we trade off now for then? Do I try to find ways to give up something that seems basic to my well-being now, but I fear will wreak havoc later? And what is my knowing about future possibilities based on, given how medical knowledge keeps changing while my ability to understand such changes in knowledge seems to diminish? Are such trajectories part of how we are "made to become so"? If what made us flourish will also make us decay, are there aspects of our bodies in the debilities of old age that will lead us to flourish?

I study Buddhism, particularly Theravada Buddhism, so I often turn to see what that tradition has to offer for topics such as this. Buddhaghosa, one of the greatest thinkers in Theravada, discusses aging in his *Visuddhimagga*, an important manual on thought and practice for monks, written in fifth-century Sri Lanka. Buddhaghosa says aging has "the characteristic of maturing (ripening) material instances." He continues, "Its function is to lead on towards." This is a strange statement. Nyanamoli, the translator of this sentence, added to it: Buddhaghosa wrote, "Its function is to lead on towards," and then Nyanamoli added, "their termination." But Buddhaghosa did not say that. He said that aging's function is to lead on towards. The sentence stops there. Buddhaghosa's next sentence continues talking about aging, "It is manifested as a loss of newness without the loss of individual essence, like oldness in a paddy." An older rice paddy produces rice that takes more water to cook. It will be less useful as seed and so on, but it looks the same. Buddhaghosa is using an example he knows. "Its proximate cause is matter that is maturing, (ripening)." This is said with reference to material aging, evident through alteration (he uses the example of teeth, as they are broken and so on). But there is also aging of immaterial things: our mind, our emotions, which have no such visible alteration. He calls this hidden aging. Here Buddhaghosa could be reflecting on what I was saying: our experience of aging is part of aging, too. He goes on to name a third category of aging, called "incessant aging." This is aging as found in earth, water, rocks, the moon, and the sun. Throughout this passage, Buddhaghosa implies that nothing in the world is exempt from aging.[24]

In this brief passage, Buddhaghosa talks about three kinds of aging: visible aging, hidden aging, and incessant aging. This division into three reminds me of another occasion in which Buddhaghosa divides an idea into three. In discussing the First Noble Truth, ("all this is suffering"), he immediately moves to discussing three kinds of suffering.[25] The word in Pali for suffering is *dukkha*. Buddhaghosa calls the first kind of suffering *dukkha-dukkha* or suffering-suffering. He is talking about visible suffering, which includes what we feel. There is another kind of suffering that is not so obvious, what he calls "suffering in change." Pleasant feelings are a "cause for suffering arising when they change."[26] We are happy now, so we do not feel suffering, but we will when our mood or situation changes. It refers to the suffering that comes with change. The third kind of suffering is conditionality—the very fact of our being is suffering in itself. With this third kind of suffering, Buddhaghosa is saying that suffering is not only an experience, and not only what we feel, it is what we are. This parallels his analysis of aging, of the incessant leading on towards. His categories for aging—visible, hidden, incessant—are here with suffering. Leading on towards.

Buddhaghosa obviously is not Cicero, bubbling with optimism. He does not avoid: he is willing to say old age is suffering, and yet, also participating in something beyond the aches and pains we feel. Buddhaghosa says, along with much of the Buddhist tradition, that suffering is a teacher second only to the Buddha himself. If old age is suffering and suffering is a teacher second only to the Buddha himself, what are we learning? As Péguy wrote, it is "a lesson no school teaches, that secret of what it means."

When I am with my mother, simply watching her in her everyday life, often I think "she's like this, this is what is happening to her." Then I remember a passage in the poem by the Mumbai poet Arun Kolatkar about his pilgrimage to the pilgrimage site in Jejari. He describes riding to the pilgrimage site on a bus with the curtains closed (intercity buses in India often close curtains so people can rest). He cannot see out the side window or the front, but he can see what is going on outside by looking at the reflection on the eyeglasses of the person next to him. He is catching a glimpse in the reflection of what this other person sees, but he is seeing it sideways.[27] I see something sideways when I am near my mother. I cannot see what she sees, but she is not keeping a secret in any particular or intentional way.

With Adorno, with the Buddha, with Buddhaghosa, we see that ideas reflecting on old age teach us something important about our lives now. I heard Bill Moyers on the radio recently. Someone asked him what he planned on doing next. To paraphrase, he said: I am seventy-three— there are fewer minutes on the clock so I want to spend time with my grandchildren and I don't want to do things like this. Somehow aging puts us in a protective space in which we start to determine what is important.

The language of "fewer minutes on the clock" points out that extreme old age as well as aging is hard to see. We have to have recourse to seeing aging and old age as what we imagine they are approximate to. We approximate when we say that extreme old age is close to death and therefore it has a flavor of death, which might not always be present. We approximate when we liken extreme old age to childhood. My mother broke her arm in the winter of 2008, and the doctor caring for her said, "your body is like a child's and so we need to take extra special precautions with it." Thankfully, he did not say to her you are like a child, even though we often do treat extremely old people as if they were children. Still, in explaining his care for her, my mother's doctor, an excellent physician, found himself approximating her aging body to something that in many other ways we would expect to be quite unlike it.

Again, what might extreme old age with all of its suffering teach? Adorno says that in looking at extreme old age we learn about a failure of contemporary cultures—the lack of resources in our contemporary cultures for making sense of what it means to live for so long, as increasing numbers now do around the world even as changes in society also frequently undermine once-traditional patterns of respect and support for the aged. Instead of routinely engaging aged people with the expectation that they have wisdom, we seem to associate old age, and especially extreme old age, less and less with categories such as wisdom. Old people, insofar as they become aged and too weak to preserve their own lives, are turned into objects of science, the science of gerontology as it is called. Adorno, in criticizing our cultures, has also said we turn old people into children as if they have a second minority.[28]

As well as a failure of our contemporary cultures, we also see a failure of possibility in how we reflect on extreme old age. Someone my age or younger might say that extreme old age is concerned with the wholeness of life, reflecting back on life, making sense of it, creating a narrative of it. When my mother turned ninety, we collected photographs and mementos from throughout her life. We thought she would enjoy looking through them. She did have some pleasure in it, but there was also disinterest, as if she was saying, "this is my high school diploma, but it is not me." She had little interest in telling a narrative around it or the other pieces. Later that same weekend when her family had gathered to celebrate her birthday with her, I was on the telephone in her living room making travel plans with someone. She was listening to my end of the conversation and said after I hung up, "I didn't know you were going to that place." I teased her, saying, "Didn't your mother teach you not to eavesdrop?" She replied, "How am I supposed to learn things if I don't eavesdrop?"

In this paper, I am eavesdropping on my mother and trying to see if I learn things, important things about being human. Before seeing my mother in her nineties, I assumed that someone in extreme old age would be someone who is not going to learn new things, not interested in learning new things, and more content to look back on what they have done and learned over the years. Instead I have learned from my mother that she is still looking, still trying to learn new things in the position she finds herself. But it seems that she is not particularly interested in learning about what it means to be ninety. She knows.

In concluding, I would like to return to that passage of Adorno's that I quoted above in which he talks about the immeasurable sadness in the decline of very old people that erodes the hope of "*non confundar*, of something which will be preserved from death." Adorno continues with comments that certainly do not describe my mother's life now but they do describe a feared reality:

> Because especially if one loves them one becomes so aware of the decrepitude of that part of them which one would like to regard as the immortal that one can hardly imagine what it is to be left over from such a poor, infirm creature which is no longer identical with itself. Thus very old people who are really reduced to what Hegel would call their mere abstract existence, those who have defied death longest, are precisely the ones who most strongly awaken the idea of absolute annulment. Nevertheless, this experience of death that is something fortuitous and external, rather like an illness one has been infected with without knowing its source, does contain a moment connected with the autonomy of mind. It is that because the mind has wrested itself so strongly from what we really are, has made itself so autonomous, this in itself gives rise to a hope that mere existence might not be everything.[29]

Throughout this essay I have emphasized that there is a strange hope in the gap between what I think my mother experiences and sees as she changes and what I see—in my mother's case, I have to be careful not to see the changes that are happening to her in ways that distort what she actually is experiencing. Above all, I have to acknowledge that she is happier than I can ever remember her being. Adorno's comments here remind us that there are other cases, particular cases, where people are losing mental faculties, physical capabilities, and the persons who love them are painfully aware in a different way of the gap between what the person once was and what they are now. This is still, however, from the vantage point not of the person experiencing it but the person looking at it.

Adorno continues by saying what happens with a person looking at the extremely old person is a "paradoxical form of hope" to which he connects "the very curious persistence of the idea of immortality."[30] There is the look and the wish: I don't want you to go. I want you to come back. I want you always to be the way you used to be. I hope for your immortality.

In terms of our theme, "rethinking the human," however we may come to understand ourselves as human, we will want always to recall this very human capability to hope for what we know is impossible—in Péguy's variant, the wish that my son will be happy even though I know there has never been a person happy.

Now let me give my mother the last word. I told her right after the conference in which this paper was first given that I had written this paper, but I only told her the title, "The Secret of a Woman of Ninety." She grinned and said, "Is it about me?" I said, "Yes, in part." Then she said, "I'm glad you think there is something worth thinking about ninety."

Truly there is.

NOTES

1. The appearance of this essay in this volume is only due to the extraordinary efforts and patience of Susan Lloyd McGarry and J. Michelle Molina and I would like to express my gratitude for all they have done. I am also grateful to Preeti Chopra, Janet Gyatso, and Donald Swearer for their comments and encouragement on this essay.

2. For an excellent analysis of this essay, "Clio—Dialogue de l'histoire et de l'âme païenne," and a translation of part of it, see Annette Aronowicz, "The Secret of the Man of Forty," *History and Theory* 32 (1993): 101–118. The material quoted here is from her translation of Péguy's essay in that article.

3. Ibid., 117–118.

4. Ibid., 118.

5. Ibid., 101.

6. Ibid., 102.

7. *Non confundar* is a notion commonly used by Adorno in his reflections on works of art, which makes this use in reference to the aged person especially noteworthy. The phrase can translated as "let me not be troubled" and is probably taken from the Christian phrase, *Non confundar in aeturnum* ("Let me not be troubled in eternity"; or as translated in the 1662 Book of Common Prayer "let me not be confounded"; see http://www.cpdl.org/wiki/index.php/Te_Deum).

8. Theodor Adorno, *Metaphysics: Concept and Problems* (Stanford: Stanford University Press, 2002), 135.

9. Helen Small, *The Long Life* (Oxford: Oxford University Press, 2007). I am deeply indebted to the work of Small throughout this essay.

10. I draw on here the discussion of Cicero's *De Senectute* in Small, *The Long Life*, 7–10.

11. Montaigne as quoted in Small, *The Long Life*, 9.

12. Any basic introduction to Buddhism will include a discussion of the Buddha's Four Noble Truths. Especially recommended is Phra Prayudh Payutto's introduction, *Buddhadhamma: Natural Laws and Values for Life* (translated by Grant Olson, Albany: SUNY Press, 1995). See especially this comment on page 167: "These Truths are related to the actual lives of all people . . . [and] constitute a central principle linked to our lives; they are really the story of our lives."

13. Life expectancy in Zimbabwe dropped from an average of sixty years in 1990 to forty-four years in 2000; it did improve slightly by 2007 by rising to forty-five. Figures are from a search of the database accessible from the World Health Organization website, www.who.int/whosis/en/index.html, conducted on October 30, 2009.

14. I use Zimbabwe as an example because my mother, Nell Hallisey, had developed a special concern for the people of Zimbabwe through her following news reports, a concern which still continues.

15. See Yukio Mishima's *The Sea of Fertility: A Cycle of Four Novels*, containing the volumes, *Spring Snow, Runaway Horses, The Temple of Dawn, The Decay of the Angel*, trans. Michael Gallagher (New York: Knopf, 1973). Quotations

are from the paperback versions (New York: Vintage, 1990) other details the same, *Runaway Horses*, 6.

16. Richard Ford, *The Lay of the Land* (New York: Knopf, 2006). The quotation is taken from a Vintage Books edition (New York: Vintage, 2007), 54.

17. See Edward Said, *On Late Style* (New York: Pantheon Books, 2006) and Adorno, *Metaphysics,* previously cited.

18. I would like to thank Dennis Hirota for emphasizing to me the significance of this difference in age for appreciating Shinran and Dogen as Buddhist thinkers.

19. For a translation of *Kyogyoshinsho*, see *The Collected Works of Shinran*, transl. Dennis Hirota, Hisao Inagaki, Michio Tokunaga, and Ryushin Uryuzu (Kyoto: Jodo Shinshu Hongwanji-Ha, 1997), Vol I, 1–292.

20. Amida, (Japanese; or Amitabha, in Sanskrit) is the center of devotion and practice for the schools of Pure Land Buddhism in East Asia, including Shinran's Jodo Shinshu ("True Pure Land School") in Japan. According to the account of Amitabha found in some Buddhist scriptures such as the *Sukhavativyuhasutra* and central to Shinran's understanding of the Buddhist path, Amitabha took a series of vows in his preparation to become a Buddha. Most important among these vows for Shinran, and the one assumed here, is the one in which Amida vowed to save anyone who called on him "with faith." In Shinran's thought, it is the "inconceivable working" of Amida's vow which is the effective mechanism of the salvation of persons, mired as we are "in blind passions and karmic evil." See, s.v. "Eighteenth Vow," and s.v. "Primal Vow," in the "Glossary of Shin Buddhist Terms," in *The Collected Works of Shinran*, Vol. II.

21. See in particular, Shinran, Letter V [On *Jinen-Honi*] written in 1258 in "Lamp for the Latter Ages (*Mattosho*)" in *The Collected Works of Shinran*, transl. Dennis Hirota et al, Vol. I, 530.

22. Simone de Beauvoir, *La Viellesse*, quoted in Small, Long Life, 13.

23. See for example the 2009 actuarial tables for the Office of the Actuary for Washington State, available on their website at http://osa.leg.wa.gov/Actuarial_Services/Actuarial_Information/Life_Expect_tables.htm where life expectancy for women stays at three years whether they are 95 or 102, compared to earlier ages where life expectancy drops a year for each year in age.

24. See Bhadantacariya Buddhaghosa, *The Path of Purification: Visuddhimagga*, trans. Bhikku Nyanamoli originally published (Colombo: R. Semage, 1956); quotations from reprint (Seattle: BPS Pariyatti Edition, 1999), 450 (XIV, 68). All quotations in this paragraph are from the same section.

25. Ibid., 505 (XVI, 34–35).

26. Ibid.

27. Arun Kolatkar, *Jejuri* (Bombay: Clearing House, 1976), 3. New edition with an introduction by Amit Chaudhuri was printed as a New York Review of Books Classic in 2005.

28. Adorno, *Metaphysics*, 106.

29. Ibid., 135.

30. Ibid.

Against Universals: The Dialects of (Women's) Human Rights and Human Capabilities

Lila Abu-Lughod [1]

I would like to recount a recent personal experience to introduce some thoughts on a key issue in discussions of "the human," the idea of universals. I will take up the problem of invoking universality in two dialects of humanity that have become "strong languages"[2] in the last part of the twentieth century and that show no signs of giving up their institutional and imaginative power in the twenty-first: human rights and human development. Since the 1990s, liberal feminists have found these languages useful and adopted them in the form of *women's* human rights and *women's* human development. As an anthropologist who works among people, including women, in the Muslim Middle East, a part of the world represented as particularly lacking in these basics of humanity, I find these languages problematic. After telling the story and then analyzing the sleights of hand entailed when "universals" are defended, I offer an alternative model for thinking about humans that does not depend on flawed oppositions between the universal and the particular, the global and the local, or universalism versus cultural relativism. This model is kinship—not naturalized, cerebralized, or romanticized, but recognized as power-laden, productive, social, and ambivalent.[3]

A Kind of Kinship

At first we overshot the driveway. I was confused by a new structure that obscured the old house. I still had not become used to the gaudy two-story structure that my old house had become in the past eight years or so since the Haj's sons had married and started their own families, swelling the household. Turning back, we drove slowly down the bumpy lane and through the large metal gates into the empty walled yard, familiar from my many years of living there in the 1970s and 1980s, even though enlarged now to accommodate the sons' cars.

The Haj's oldest son—whose fresh scar from open heart surgery for a congenital heart condition had traumatized me when I was a young graduate student living with this family in the late 1970s—came out to greet me. His face looked puffy. Was he unshaven? I searched his eyes. Were they red?

Then I saw the women crowding the doorway to greet me and I hurried in. I was surprised to find not just the Haj's two wives but his sisters, one of whom lived in Alamein, out along the Northwest Coast of Egypt where the Awlad 'Ali Bedouin lived. Along with all these new daughters-in-law I barely knew were several of his daughters, now married and no longer living at home. They all looked as if they had not slept well.

Was my foreboding justified? About a month earlier, in New York, I'd had a dream about the Haj, a dream that had jolted me from sleep. I was worried. I was returning for a visit without having been able to contact my old friends for more than a year. I knew that the Haj, born the same year as my father, would be seventy-nine. It had been seven years since I lost my father. A photo from three years ago that was part of the revolving slideshow on my computer screen showed the Haj standing with his arm around my daughter, then twelve. Whenever it came up, I looked hard at him, noticing that he was old and thin, despite the twinkle in his eye and his warm smile.

The women saw the silent questioning in my eyes and told me right away that the Haj was in the hospital. He had taken a turn for the worse a few days ago, a week or so after they had brought him home from a month of treatment in Alexandria. They had just rushed him back to the hospital. But he was okay. The Haj's right arm and leg were paralyzed. He could talk, they explained, but "his tongue is heavy." He had had a stroke. He had refused to take his blood pressure medicine, instead having his camel herds brought nearby so that, back to his roots and his youth, he could drink camel milk every morning. He was one of the last Bedouin to hold on to his camel herds, symbols of their past life. Just before the stroke, despite his high blood pressure and diabetes, he had agreed to mediate a tense dispute between two groups. The women blamed his stroke on this event.

His doctor, the women reported, said that he would be able to come home soon from the hospital. But we were in suspended time. A telephone call to the hospital (and the Haj's younger son and nephew who had spent the night with him) confirmed that they were not sure when he would be discharged. I said I had to go see him.

After the young men returned from Friday prayers, we set off in two cars—two sons, a nephew, the Haj's two youngest daughters (whose births I remembered and who now startled me with their beauty and confidence, not to mention the swishing elegance of the newly fashionable black robes and face veils they put on when it was time to go), and myself. Later everyone would ask me if I had come because I had heard the news. Later they told each other that I had dreamt of him. Later they told me that when the Haj heard that I had come, he insisted that they should let him go home right away.

Some intense days followed—days of aching affection, forced cheeriness, and hidden tears. Days when I had to watch this extraordinary man, now returned home, reduced to physical helplessness, surrounded by women and young men lifting him, feeding him, hovering around him. No longer in intense conversation, no longer telling the young people what to do, no longer sitting cross-legged in dignity. These were days when I was reminded of how close families were in this community. Married daughters arrived and held his young grandchildren close to his face so each could plant a kiss on his check as he turned feebly toward them. Other daughters propped him up in bed and fed him by hand bits of fish and salad, healthy food that his diabetes forced him to eat when he'd rather have his old desert food of dates and butter. People came into the room to see him, encouraging him, babying him. He would whisper for the young men, his sons and nephews. What he wanted from them was cigarettes. They delayed as long as possible but he persisted.

I could not make out what he was saying most of the time, this man who had been so articulate and clear. He had told me stories and history, taught me poetry, and explained to me so much of Bedouin life from customary law to the dynamics of his own marriages. As I sat next to his bed (everyone insisting since my time was short and this visit precious that I have this special place), I held his lifeless hand, looked at his grizzled face and rumpled clothes, and strained to understand him when he tried to speak. After a life of respect for his gifts as a judge, a talker, and from a young age a charismatic leader and later "elder," the Haj now lay there quietly in bed. I tried to reminisce with him; he followed me with his eyes.

We had a living bond that reminded him, me, and everyone there, of almost a lifetime together. It brought back the past. The intensity, for all of us, was heightened because of the moment when that connection began—many years ago when we were all younger. I had been a shy twenty-six year old with strong feelings, a desperate urge to understand their world as I lived in it, and an unknown life ahead of me. His wives had been in the midst of the earthy pleasures and exasperations of having babies, raising children, and dealing with a husband who was complicated, demanding, and special. Then he had been in his prime, driving all over Bedouin territory to do deals and handle disputes, in demand, restless, on a bridge between a past tougher life that included smuggling goods across irrelevant national boundaries, recovering landmines left over from World War II, and managing his camel herds, and a future full of real estate deals and agribusiness, still young enough to remember lost loves.

Our human bond was real, across so many divides that contemporary discourses about culture consider fundamental. Divides which seem impossible to bridge in the discourses of "multiculturalism and empire," to borrow Wendy Brown's felicitous phrase.[4] It was across the divide of culture and religion, despite our mutual understanding of me as of Arab and Muslim origin even if living in ways that were strange to them. Religion was crucial for the Haj and this Bedouin community in every aspect of their lives. Not for me. For various reasons, I never got the habit of religion; I got the habit of humanism. To be a humanist is to understand that for most humans what we call religious traditions are deeply meaningful. I respect that meaningfulness and I recognize the historical power of religious practice, debate, and identity. I found in anthropology the perfect discipline for someone in my existential state: it sanctions respect and enables understanding without demanding full participation.

I can and do participate in most ways when in the Haj's world. I speak—or try my best to speak—their dialect of Arabic and even the strong language of Islam that is theirs. Everyone entering the bedroom to greet the Haj voiced the prayer that God would make him well. His response was always "Thanks/Praise be to God." I too talked about God's power and God's will and entreated God to heal him. People say these words in such situations. I could only say the same things, translating my inchoate hopes and concern for him into this recognizable language. Maybe this is all it takes to place us in the same world, if the humanity of an already shared life, a real connection, is there.

There was a second divide between the Haj and me—the kind of vexed divide that has been made emblematic of the unbridgeable relations between the civilized and the barbaric, the enlightened and the backward: the divide between those who profess women's rights and equality and those who do not. Let me give you one more detail from this story of my return visit. When I finally had to wrench myself away to go back to Cairo, we all knew the goodbyes might be final. The Haj gestured for his son to come close. Protective as ever, I realized later that he had instructed him to make sure he got me safely into the minibus and stressed to the driver that he must watch out for me. A little later, I saw the Haj fumbling to reach his good hand into the top of his robes. Only his wife and daughter were in the room now. They didn't know what he was doing and kept asking, "What do you want?" But I knew. I knew he was looking for his wallet, still wanting to give his young "daughter" some money, to take care of her, to make sure she didn't want for anything. I was a successful academic, a married mother of teenagers, a world traveler. I was a specialist in gender studies. Even when I had lived with them for my dissertation research in the late 1970s and early 1980s, despite being poor and having been entrusted to them by my father, I had been pursuing a PhD and living away from home, ultimately independent as no young unmarried women were in his community. In that moment when he fumbled for the wallet that was not there, I felt the protected and loved (and loving) daughter he saw in me. It pained me to see his masculine dignity compromised—for he had no wallet and no control over things.[5]

Here was a man who had not allowed his four youngest daughters to go to university, for fear that something might happen to them so far from home (though he probably also used a complex calculus that included such facts as that they had not attended good enough high schools to go to top faculties and that none of his sons had attended university). Here was a man who lived in a household where women covered themselves in public and kept their very respectable distance from men. Here was a man who had married several wives. True, the Haj had recognized the talents and educational successes of his daughters by arranging for them to marry men who, though perhaps lacking in family status or great wealth, were educated men rather than cousins. True he had shown his love and respect for his senior wife in trusting her in all matters and, only a few months earlier, enabling her to realize her dream of performing the pilgrimage to Mecca. True he supported all his wives and children well and tried to be fair. And true he had sheltered women whose family situations were bad and had used his moral authority to enforce their rights to good treatment by husbands or kin. But no one here had heard of the *UN Convention on the Elimination of All Forms of Discrimination Against Women*. This was not a society in which "gender equity" was part of the vocabulary of everyday life, though women defended fiercely a variety of rights. Here was a society that feminists might label "patriarchal" by pointing to the way women and girls were ensconced in family, though I would point out in response that men and boys were equally so.[6]

And yet the Haj and I were able to be close, through a kind of kinship and a mutual recognition of complexities. His playful affection for his children reminded me of my father's. Both were men with big public lives—my father's in the international Palestinian community and the Haj's in the Western Desert of Egypt. I loved his girls, his daughters, and they loved me in their own ways. Some confided in me as an older sister, about the anxieties and medical interventions of infertility. Others were connected to me metonymically. One had as background on her cellphone a photograph I had taken twenty years ago of her father playfully hugging her when she was just two. Older women teased me, and asked earnestly about the health and news of every member of my family as their way to connect us. I was stunned by how many details they remembered about me. I empathized when the Haj's wife moaned as I massaged her aching lower back and we both laughed when she complained, "O my knees!" as she stood up. We recognized this refrain from twenty-five years ago when I used to make her effervescent vitamin drinks to help with her indigestion in pregnancy.[7]

Shared times, a life lived in common, intensely for a couple of years, and stretching over thirty years. These bridged the divides, despite our different worlds, possibilities, knowledges, and aspirations. My experience is not unique; I suspect we have all experienced something of this bridging. Perhaps every intimate relationship involves this bridging. The question is what we can learn about "the human" from such personal experiences of kinship that develop through intense living together and that do not demand sameness.

The Language of Universals as a Dialect

In *Writing Women's Worlds*, my second ethnography of the Awlad 'Ali Bedouin of Egypt's Western Desert, I argued that we needed to write ethnographies of the particular. Even if we were theoretically skeptical of its claims, we needed to practice humanism—to build on the moral force of a philosophy that could unite us across cultures, languages, religions, and their political manipulations.[8] I called this a "tactical humanism." In writing about the complex stories of these Bedouin individuals I'd come to know intimately, I was "writing against culture." Culture, I argued, was a term that tended to fix difference and homogenize groups of individuals.

I would still defend those ideas, though I would not now write in the same way about the communities and individuals I have come to know in Egypt as I did in that ethnographic experiment. Instead, in this essay I want to push further the analytical issues raised in that book by examining closely those discourses that produce and reproduce the sense of cultural divide even when they pretend not to by invoking something called the "human." I have shared this story about the Haj to introduce a critique of the positions that many liberal humanists take with regard to multiculturalism and social relations in what we call "our globalized world." What disturb me are the normative assumptions that seem inevitable within the frame of secular liberalism. I will trace these assumptions in two discourses about the human that are central in the academic and political debates in which I am currently most involved as someone who researches the politics of gender in Arab Muslim societies.

Feminists writing in the last couple of decades, as noted above, have piggybacked on two hegemonic languages of the human in order to make claims for women: human rights and human development. Feminists working in the international arena have waged a successful campaign to declare women's rights human rights. The philosopher Martha Nussbaum has spent much of her later career taking the discourse of human development to questions of what she calls "sex and justice." The rhetorical fault-line in both of these "dialects of humanity" is a binary distinction between the universal and the local or the particular. This distinction is twinned with another: the universal versus the partisan.

What exactly is meant when the "universal" is invoked, whether in the *Universal Declaration of Human Rights of the United Nations* (UN),[9] that authorizing document for the discourses and practices of human rights, or in insisting that we must promote—and judge countries and societies on the basis of their success in enabling the functioning of—"human capabilities" defined as universal? I think we would all agree that it is one or more of the following:

1. something that should or does apply or should or does exist uniformly in a global/geographic sense, as opposed to something locally specific or selectively applied;

2. something that is neutral, in that it belongs "to everyone and anyone" and in a sense, therefore, to no one in particular—the opposite of something partisan that favors one group or grows out of its interests; or

3. as in ethical discourses on human societies, practices and values, where applying universal standards is regularly contrasted to a stance called cultural relativism.

As we can see, the "universal" is always understood through a distinction from another term. It is seen as the stronger, the more encompassing, the more general term. Interestingly, it is also the more abstract term, considered to stand above particulars. In moral terms it is presented as that which should structure all instantiations. But this is a disavowal of its particularity. The language of universality is actually just a dialect. This can be illustrated by analyzing some of the key texts about gender justice that traffic in discourses of universality and the human.[10]

A good place to begin is the regularly invoked *UN Universal Declaration of Human Rights* (UDHR).[11] We find here that foundational statement: "All human beings are born free and equal in dignity and rights." We know that the declaration is tautological; we know, as Slaughter explores in *Human Rights Inc.*,[12] that it both claims to tell us what everyone already knows and what everyone should know; we know that it is meant to reflect universal (shared) ideals and to be applied universally (everywhere) but that it is enforceable only by nation-states and more often recognized selectively in the breach. We know that it was produced over a three-year period ending in 1948 by a limited number of diplomats and statesmen and women from the limited number of member nations of the newly formed United Nations. We know that though it claims a genealogy in the Magna Carta, the French Declaration of the Rights of Man and the Citizen, and the American Declaration of Independence, it was a product of a particular post–World War II moment when most of the world was actually still under colonial control.[13] We know that the American Anthropological Association "warned the United Nations against adopting a universal bill of rights that did not attend to cultural particularities" in its own statement written in response to the 1947 UNESCO call for contributions to help with the drafting of the Universal Declaration.[14] And we recognize that, as Spivak has noted, even the claims to universality pronounced through offering official translations into many non-European languages should be dismissed since these are only "symbolic gestures of equality." She explains, "No one who doesn't know a hegemonic European language will have any idea what's going on in these so-called translations."[15]

Sally Engle Merry's ethnography of the translation of human rights discourse into local contexts and, even more interestingly, of the development and workings of subsequent international instruments of women's rights beginning with the *Convention on the Elimination of all Forms of Discrimination against Women* adopted by the United Nations General Assembly in December 1979,[16] lays out how such international documents that claim the status of universality are hammered out in social settings in which participants, who themselves live in at least two local places at the same time (the UN being just as local a place as their countries of origin), navigate an "English-speaking, largely secular, universalistic, law-governed culture, organized around the formal equality of nations and their economic and political inequality."[17] The power of her analysis of the transnational movement against gender violence lies in the way she undermines the opposition between universalism and particularism by revealing how the very instruments of a putatively universal international law are themselves part of a located culture, with its own transnational social spaces, rather than existing above any particular social world. Or as some other anthropologists of human rights put it, where "the pursuit of human rights is approached itself as a cultural process."[18] Merry does not accuse such documents of being Western, as more simplistic arguments about cultural imperialism might. Instead, she takes very seriously the fact that these conventions and instruments of human rights are socially produced in particular times and places and with particular personnel operating in a particular transnational culture. She brilliantly traces how this sociality shapes them and in turn how such instruments are deployed in specific social fields.

The feminist legal scholar Catherine MacKinnon, who invokes universal rights in campaigns against pornography and rape, instead locates the culture of such documents not in the actual meeting rooms of the UN but in a worldwide patriarchy in which international institutions and nation-states participate. Her plaintive question, "When will women be human?" is a challenge not only to the failure to apply the *Universal Declaration of Human Rights* universally but also to its partial or exclusionary vision of the human. After melodramatically cataloguing in the first person plural all the abuses women in particular suffer, she writes, "Women need full human status in social reality. For this, the Universal Declaration of Human Rights must see the ways women distinctively are deprived of human rights as a deprivation of humanity . . . . for human rights to be universal, both the reality it [the UDHR] challenges and the standard it sets need to change."[19]

MacKinnon's *Are Women Human?*[20] is the first of three well-known texts on the "human rights" side in which equity is the key term, the political/legal the key register, and universalism the demand. I would also like to discuss Charlotte Bunch's "Women's Rights as Human Rights"[21] and Susan Moller Okin's *Is Multiculturalism Bad for Women?*[22]

Charlotte Bunch, the feminist who articulated, if not spearheaded, the transnational movement in the 1990s to assert "women's rights as human rights," has mobilized some of the same arguments as MacKinnon. She asserts that women's issues should not be treated as separate issues; they are actually just neglected aspects of global agendas for human rights and development. Governments should be committed to women's equality as a basic human right. Like MacKinnon, she asks why degrading aspects of women's lives have not been considered human rights issues. Sex discrimination and violence against women, she charges, had been excluded until the 1990s from the human rights agenda because people had failed to see the oppression of women as political—as politically constructed to serve patriarchal interests, ideology, and institutions; instead they took them as natural.[23] Both Bunch and MacKinnon call for a universally applied standard of gender equality through appeal to the universal rights of the human.

One of the most debated statements on the need to make gender equity a universal social priority is Susan Moller Okin's essay attacking multiculturalism. This liberal political theorist pits feminism against any and all arguments for group or cultural rights. In her essay, she lines up the liberal ideal of sex equity, defined as the possibility for women to "live as fulfilling and as freely chosen lives as men can"[24] (which she grants is also not fully realized in liberal states) against "culture," which as Wendy Brown has shown, she seems to locate only outside the West— only *outside* liberal states.[25] Although Okin does not appeal explicitly to universals, as do the other two, her argument rests on the assumption that liberal culture is the acultural norm and thus should be the universal standard by which to measure societies, especially the barbarians outside the gates in thrall to their cultures (now come to live within the gates as immigrants). Moreover, in her denunciation of all cultures as basically patriarchal, as involving men's control over women, Okin notes that much discrimination against women occurs in the private sphere. From her analysis of this as a problem, we can see clearly the operation of liberal values as the *universal* standard. Discrimination in home and family is especially pernicious, she argues, because such practices "are never likely to emerge in public, where courts can enforce their rights and political theorists can label such practices as illiberal *and therefore* unjustified violations of women's physical or mental integrity" (my emphasis).[26] As Brown has objected, drawing on a long line of feminist critiques of liberalism, the public sphere may not be neutral or any better than the private sphere. Brown asks, "[W]hat if liberalism itself harbors male dominance, what if male superordination is inscribed in liberalism's core values of liberty—rooted in autonomy and centered on self-interest—and equality—defined as sameness and confined to the public sphere?"[27]

Universal Capabilities Also a Dialect

The other major strand of liberal feminist thought that invokes universality is represented best by Martha Nussbaum, the most prominent proponent of the human capabilities approach in women and development. In a series of essays and books, she has argued that the best way to promote gender justice is to insist that there are basic human capabilities and that our task is to reform societies and nation-states so that they will promote human flourishing in terms of these capabilities. Early on, she describes herself as subscribing to an Aristotelian position on "the proper function of government, according to which its task is to make available to each and every member of the community the basic, necessary conditions of the capability to choose and live a fully good human life, with respect to each of the major human functions included in that fully good life."[28] In a sense, her project is to extend this to nation-states under a modern international regime of governance. In her most accessible work, *Women and Human Development*, especially the section titled "In Defense of Universal Values," she distinguishes her approach from the rights approach.[29] As she explains, ". . . capabilities . . . have a very close relationship to human rights, as understood in contemporary international discussions. In effect they cover the terrain covered by both the so-called first-generation rights (political and civil liberties) and the so-called second-generation rights (economic and social rights) . . . . Because the language of rights is well established, the defender of capabilities needs to show what is added by this new language."[30] For her, the most important advantage is that this language "bypasses the troublesome debate" about the derivation of "rights" talk from the Western Enlightenment. The capabilities approach, she claims, "is not strongly linked to one particular cultural and historical tradition, as the language of rights is believed to be."[31]

Nussbaum may be correct that the capabilities approach has not been tainted with its association with the West in the same way that human rights, despite multiple attempts to locate such rights within particular and "non-Western" traditions (as evidenced in "The International Islamic Declaration of Human Rights" or "The Cairo Declaration of Human Rights in Islam" or the Islamic Human Rights Commission in Iran).[32] Her continually revised list of "human functional capabilities" is divided, in the 2000 work, into ten categories: Life; Bodily Health; Bodily Integrity; Senses, Imagination, and Thought; Emotions; Practical Reason; Affiliation; Other Species; Play; and Control over One's Environment. To convey both the universalistic rhetoric she deploys and the extreme cultural particularity of the elements she presents as universal, one needs to examine the ways she actually describes these human capabilities. Talal Asad has quoted the most blatantly value-laden of these in his essay, "Redeeming the Human in Human Rights."[33] He did not bother to unpack it, however, perhaps because he considered the cultural and class particularities of this view of the human so self-evident. The capability in question is that of "Senses, Imagination, and Thought." Here is Nussbaum's description:

> Being able to use the senses, to imagine, think, and reason—and to do these things in a "truly human" way, a way informed and cultivated by an adequate education, including, but by no means limited to, literacy and basic mathematical and scientific training. Being able to use imagination and thought in connection with experiencing and producing self-expressive works and events of one's own choice, religious, literary, musical, and so forth. Being able to use one's mind in ways protected by guarantees of freedom of expression with respect to both political and artistic speech, and freedom of religious exercise. Being able to search for the ultimate meaning of life in one's own way. Being able to have pleasurable experiences, and to avoid non-necessary pain.[34]

Where can we begin to tease out the modern Western liberal assumptions about individualism, autonomy, and secularism embedded in this "consensual" and thus allegedly universalist description? From the valuation of mathematics to the individualistic voluntarism of "self-expressive" works "of one's own choice," from the presumption that education cultivates the imagination to the abstract idea of having "a mind" that one can "use," from the asocial and ahistorical presumption that a human can search for meaning *in his or her own way* as if not embedded in and produced by a family and community and world position that create subjective desires if not the subject him or herself, to the simple assessment that pleasure is good and pain evil that ignores the paradoxes of voluntary pain whether in religious or initiatory rituals (medieval and contemporary, European or Native American) or in sexual practices, this statement of universals is mired in particulars and is a partisan vision of the human. As Asad notes, "It is itself a thick account of what being human is—and one that underpins human rights."[35]

An anthropologist would have to take issue with the "universality" of most of the values promoted: "Being able to live one's own life and nobody else's" as if there could be "non-interference with certain choices that are especially personal and definitive of selfhood"[36] when we know that marriage, sexual expression, speech, and work are deeply structured by historically specific social and imaginative systems; "Being able to live with concern for and in relation to animals, plants, and the world of nature"[37] when anthropologists have written articles based on research in Melanesia entitled "No Nature No Culture" to highlight the cultural and historical particularity of the very concept of "nature" and have explored in many volumes, whether on totemism or hunting, the bewildering relations humans have to animals that are either "good to eat" or "good to think."[38] Most people with experience of life in other places or knowledge of human history would be likely to see how located her "frankly universalist and 'essentialist'"[39] vision of the human is, or, to use my metaphor, just how much of a local dialect this language of universals turns out to be.

Against the Language of Universals

The "silent referent"[40] for "the universal" in schemas like Okin's and Nussbaum's is an imagined and idealized liberal democracy along with a form of modern culture and reason that, through the language of universalism, it helps create while simultaneously distancing itself from the negative opposites it imaginatively locates elsewhere in the world. In the cases of liberal feminist discourses, this imagined opposite tends to be, in the specific examples in the works of these writers, the Middle East and Muslim world, South Asia, and Africa, where they melodramatically condemn veiling, child marriage, dowry death, or genital cutting. Implied in all these arguments is that it is the lives of women of the non-West, and the communities or governments that fail to support their rights or to allow them a flourishing life (in the terms defined), that are particularly deficient. Okin writes, in a much quoted passage, that "While virtually all of the world's cultures have distinctly patriarchal pasts some—mostly, though by no means exclusively, Western liberal cultures—have departed far further from them than others."[41] This is the unstated presumption of the arguments by MacKinnon, Bunch, and Nussbaum, too. The "universal" human rights of women and the free exercise of their human capabilities, it is implied, are violated less egregiously in the modern Western liberal democracies from which these North American women speak and in whose particular and "provincial" language they make their case.

So, my first argument is that we must provincialize the universal human that is the assumed ground in these dialects of women's rights as human rights or women's human capabilities. This is quite different from arguing in favor of cultural relativism, group rights, tolerance, or pluralism. Instead, I argue that we need to make a double move against universalism: one historical/anthropological, the other philosophical.

The historical/anthropological case highlights the provincialism of arguments that pit cultures against universalism (or against other cultures) and traces the genealogy of the notions of universal humanity through colonialism, among other relationships. As Leti Volpp has suggested, the very notion of culture, as mobilized by liberals, is part of the problem. Both the rights and the capabilities approaches use cultural arguments to explain minority and Third World sex-subordinating practices.[42] In doing so, they obscure the degree to which many women's problems around the world are rooted in forces beyond their individual cultures or communities—for example, in international structures of inequality, new patriarchies related to politicized religious movements, and flows of transnational capital. They direct attention away from issues affecting women that are separate from what are considered sexist cultural practices—problems that they might share with men or other classes. They position "other" women as victims rather than agents, what Ratna Kapur calls "victim subjects."[43] Meanwhile they divert our gaze from the sexism "indigenous" to the U.S., Europe, and the middle class—including domestic violence and glass ceilings. Referring to the work of philosopher Uma Narayan, who has calculated that the death of women by domestic violence in the United States is easily as numerically significant a social problem as dowry murders in India, Volpp observes that we say, "They burn their women there," but we do not say, "We shoot our women here." Only *other* women, not those in Western liberal democracies, suffer "death by culture."[44]

As Volpp adds, one should still take a critical stance towards the various forms of gender subordination. But more ethical stances require us to go beyond simplistic oppositions between us and them, women and men, Western and Third World. It is not helpful to consider culture and religion simply as obstacles to women's human rights. Assuming an automatic opposition between women's rights as universal human rights on the one hand and culture or religion as particular obstacles, on the other, blocks us from coming to more nuanced positions and solutions. The reduction of many complex issues to a simple conflict between feminism and culture/ religion prevents us from thinking about the multiple forms of feminism, the culture and social lives of women's rights and capabilities, and the long history of geopolitical entanglements among the specific groups that are represented today as so separate and incompatible, enlightened on one side and traditional and patriarchal on the other. These societies and cultures have produced and shaped each other and stand in particular relationships to each other. The divide makes no sense.

Moreover, as Anupama Rao and I have written, though the discourse of human rights became institutionalized and began to be seen as a global form of rescue in the period after the Second World War, in the aftermath of the Holocaust and with the end of imperial rule across Asia and Africa, it has a long history. Philosophies of freedom and equality, articulated during the eighteenth century, developed in the context of projects of colonization and global expansion. The abolitionist discourses of the · nineteenth century drew their inspiration from evangelical conceptions of the equality of all human beings, countering arguments about racial inferiority and barbarism that supported the institution of slavery and colonial expansion. In each of these instances, race, culture, and most importantly, religion, were characterized as impediments to modernization, deflecting attention away from the illiberal forms of governance characterizing imperial rule.[45] Invocations of universalism in the dialects of human rights and human development are, in short, part of long historical relationships among societies and cannot be taken out of context.

There is also a philosophical argument against the deployment of concepts of universal rights and capabilities. These abstract concepts create a metric by which humans, imagined as incommensurate, with their experiences in societies imagined as separate, can be lined up and compared. The concepts of universal human rights or human capabilities work as codes for naming and arranging experiences. Presenting themselves as "universal" in the sense of neutral and above any particular set of human experiences, they hide from themselves and us their very particularity and derivation. A telling illustration of the imagination of such metrics as somehow standing above particulars can be seen in Nussbaum's defense of her list as constructed from an "overlapping consensus." She argues that "people may sign on to this conception as the freestanding moral core of a political conception, without accepting any particular metaphysical view of the world, any particular comprehensive ethic or religious view, or even any particular view of the person or of human nature."[46] Thus a dialect of the human is made to appear a general language that all can speak, whatever their particular views. This ignores the common saying that "a language . . . is but a dialect backed up by an army" and that there are global institutions that seek, and have had the power, to organize the world in a particular way and to set the standards by which the lives of others are evaluated and judged.[47]

Which brings me to the stark choice that those who speak the language of human rights and capabilities often insist must be made: the moral choice between universalism or relativism. This does not do justice to the situations we confront in the world; it partakes of the obfuscations about "the universal" that I have just described. Neither in the realm of international relations nor in the sphere of the play of difference can anyone abdicate moral responsibility or judgment. How do we think about such matters as gender relations in other places without being forced to choose between supporting "universal" human values (which I have shown to be parochial) and a wishy-washy cultural relativism or worse, supporting "partisan claims"? In an essay called "Do Muslim Women Really Need Saving?" written in 2001 as the U.S. had used the saving of women from the Taliban as one of its most persuasive justifications for the invasion of Afghanistan, I argued that my rejection of such military intervention, with its colonial echoes of what Spivak famously described as "saving brown women from brown men" or what Leila Ahmed called "colonial feminism," was not based on a cultural relativism that would say that Afghans should be allowed to practice their culture.[48] Instead, I made three arguments:

- first, that we had to recognize the historical interconnections between Afghanistan and the rest of the world, including the United States, which had helped enable Afghan and Taliban "culture" and practices, not to mention political control by the latter;
- second, that any call to save Afghan women from their culture entailed violence, since in saving them from something we would also be seeking to save them to something else, presumably the allegedly "universal" culture of the human that this paper has described; and
- third, that we had to take responsibility for our part in the creation of the conditions in which issues of gender, women's priorities, and women's freedoms had taken a particular form and now could or could not be debated within Afghanistan.

The U.S. has not stood outside of Afghanistan; its funding and manipulation of political groups having been substantial and of long duration. I argued that those concerned about women's rights had the responsibility to work on U.S. policies so that they were not so devastating for people in Afghanistan, so that Afghan women could find the space and peace to be able to debate the changes they might want.

Imagining Another Dialect?

The human of human rights and human capabilities is particular. The human of secular liberalism has been historically constructed and is being disseminated through international institutions and practices so that it is, to some extent, everywhere—translated, resisted, vernacularized, invoked in political struggles, and made the standard language enforced by power. I have argued that the differences that exist in the world are grounded in different histories and the particular and shifting forms of interlinkages, historical and political and cultural, among human communities. We have made each other in so many ways. When some communities are now charged with lagging behind in granting humanity to women because of the obstacles of tradition or culture, we need to ask:

- What are the historical processes that have made certain notions of "universal" human progress seem self-evident?
- What historical processes have made the generation, imagination, and application of universal metrics of human well-being seem so normal, and so moral, both generally and in the case of women?
- Is the universal language of the human the dialect of the metropole? Of the cosmopolitan? Of the elite?[49]

Two strands in anthropology and postcolonial studies offer useful ways to move beyond the flawed discourses of cultural relativism or multicultural toleration that are usually posed as the alternatives to universalism in the moral discourses about difference. Dipesh Chakrabarty's call to provincialize Europe is not a call to cultural relativism. He insists that you cannot be a defensive nativist or charge that the qualities that define Europe as modern are simply "culture-specific." Rather, he argues, the next step is "a matter of documenting how—through what historical process—its [the European Enlightenment's] 'reason,' which was not always self-evident to everyone, has been made to look obvious far beyond the ground where it originated."[50] The qualities he writes about as defining "modern" Europe are science, Enlightenment reason, and a sense of being universal. Others have talked about how these qualities developed in the colonial theater or laboratory and thus should not be so easily seen as strictly European.[51] Chakrabarty instead urges us to look at the historical processes that have installed this "Europe," this modernity—and I would add, this universal human—everywhere. Among the most important of these processes, he argues, are both imperialism and Third World nationalism.[52] I am less concerned to explore the processes than to note that there have been processes.

Anthropology has had its own traditions of provincializing the West, though it has usually proceeded by fetishizing difference rather than historicizing it. Marcus and Fischer famously traced a tradition in anthropology of reflexive cultural critique, exemplified recently by a pamphlet by Marshall Sahlins that, based on the old Geertzian notion of "human nature as culturally informed becoming" and ranging promiscuously across the exotic cultures of the world, holds up to scrutiny the peculiar Western conception of an innate selfish human nature as "an illusion of world-anthropological proportions."[53]

We can read Saba Mahmood, an anthropologist studying women in the piety movement in Egypt, as in this tradition but pushing it further. She draws on different philosophical arguments in claiming that her work is meant to redress "the profound inability within current feminist political thought to envision valuable forms of human flourishing outside the bounds of a liberal progressive imaginary."[54] She concludes her study, ". . . what I mean to gesture at is a mode of encountering the Other which does not assume that in the process of culturally translating other lifeworlds one's own certainty about how the world should proceed can remain stable."[55]

I have long been sympathetic to this approach because my own mentor Paul Riesman had suggested in the 1970s through his work with the Fulani in West Africa the radical idea that we might learn *from* those among whom we did research. His book, *Freedom in Fulani Social Life*, centered on what he learned about freedom and interdependency from those with whom he lived in Burkino Faso, then Upper Volta.[56] In that ethnography, he included psychoanalytic insights into his own responses in the field. Riesman did not fetishize difference; he recognized the possibility of exchange, of learning about himself, and at least the momentary "existential" sharing of lives, in Michael Jackson's words.[57]

What, whether, or how much we can learn from others are open questions. However, my story of visiting the Haj and his family shows that we do learn from our experiences of sharing lives with others. I remain keenly aware of the power differences that shape the flows of such visits as mine—why it is the anthropologist who goes and comes while the "native" stays put, as Arjun Appadurai noted some time ago.[58] But I know that there is something wrong with the complacent assumption that people around the world *must* learn from "us" how to be modern and civilized, or how to measure up in the universal metric of humanity, as the dialects of women's human rights and women's human capabilities presume. Human rights and human capabilities talk is part of this "universal reason" that needs to be parochialized, not in order to dismiss it as Western or to make peace with it by asserting that other religious or cultural traditions share the same values and we can reach the same ends more authentically if we draw on those for "internal validation," as someone like An-Na'im puts it,[59] but rather, following Chakrabarty's lead, to ask what historical processes and what institutional arrangements, from nation-states to flourishing forms of transnational governance and advocacy in a global world, have installed these dialects of universality in so many places as a "universal" language and coding of the human.[60] To do so is not to deny the moral and political gains which the political or strategic uses of such dialects have enabled in various communities and parts of the world, or to discredit future benefits for many disenfranchised groups and individuals, including women who learn to use this powerful language or who, as Merry suggests, come to translate their grievances into its terms.[61] It is to know their limits; to see what they exclude; to recognize their links with institutions and geopolitical configurations of power; and to see "the scandalous aspects"[62] of our translations into this language, for all particular communities of humans including those whose "mother tongue" it might be.

My stories from Egypt about the Haj suggest that we do not actually need this mediating code to speak to each other. When I reflect on my relationship with him and his family, I am tempted to turn to another metaphor of universality that is also embedded in the language of the human. What if we took more seriously as a model not the fantasy of "universality" but the "family of man" that was imagined as part of the wishful declaration of a common humanity in the post-war period?[63] That it was called a family of "man" is only one index of its historical specificity, of course. And that the preamble of the UDHR should define members of the "human family" by their "equal and inalienable rights" is very peculiar, given our experiences of actual families. One might argue instead that families are by nature contingent and ever-changing, their dynamics volatile, their membership flexible.

Anthropologists used to study kinship. They studied the bewildering array of complex ways humans have imagined their social and emotional relations, as well as the logics by which they have organized themselves and the meaning they have given to their differences and affinities. They studied the various inclusions and exclusions of kinship; the workings of memory and amnesia. They joined psychologists and novelists in marveling at the intense emotions and sharp interactions within diverse families that shape individual experience and personhood. In recent years, feminist anthropologists have become fascinated with the forms of kinship that new reproductive technologies and organ transplantation have spawned, just as earlier they critiqued the heteronormative constructions that made us imagine families only one way or as biologically given.[64] They showed us that families are not necessarily at the core of social formations and that they are ideological constructs that differ. On the ground, every "family" is different, even the happy ones, contrary to Leo Tolstoy's famous pronouncement in the opening of *Anna Karenina*.

Eight and a half months after the visit with the Haj with which I opened this essay, I again found myself being driven up the same driveway, the yard now forlorn and empty. A telephone call from one of the Haj's daughters, her cell phone to mine, had given me the sad news that he had never recovered. The daughter, now living in a small city further west, with a son beginning a computer engineering course, had been eleven when I first came to live with them.[65] A tough girl who had taken a special interest in disciplining my unconventional forays into the men's guestroom to talk to her father's guests, she was the one to insist that I had to be told. Her mother and sisters had thought it would be too hard to hear the news when I was alone and so far away. So many women in this community had told me stories of how someone had come to get them from their marital homes, telling them a father, or brother, or mother was ill, never wanting to break the news of death until they had arrived among loved ones. If I had not had the uncanny feeling that made me come for that visit last spring, they would not have had my phone number. I marveled at the technology that could now bridge our worlds.

I was touched by this inclusion, and sad. I knew I had to go. I heard many stories about his last days. But the story about his mental sharpness that drew me up short was one about me. It seems that after I had left in early April, they had discovered what he had been trying to say when he fumbled inside his robe. His wife explained to me what I had already figured out: that he had wanted his wallet. The reason, though, was that he had had some U.S. dollars in it. Dollars were, of course, my kind of money. So perhaps his gesture was not so much the generic protective generosity of a father toward a daughter that I had imagined then but a gesture that acknowledged who I was, specifically. I was the odd daughter who was and was not like his other daughters. I came from and still lived in another place and world, even if we had become over the years part of each other's lives.

Families harbor distance and closeness, violence and love, indifference and passion. These facts make the notion of kinship an intriguing model for thinking about relations among people in the world—where family is about living together, across individual differences, in ever-changing relations not just of affiliation or affection but of dependency, struggles over authority, and ambivalence.[66]

NOTES

1. I am grateful to Janet Abu-Lughod, Tim Mitchell, J. Michelle Molina, Julienne Obadia, and Ayse Parla for helpful comments and suggestions. Don Swearer and Michael Jackson at the Harvard Center for the Study of World Religions invited me to the conference on "Rethinking the Human" that was the stimulus for reflecting on these issues. My students at Columbia University have helped me think about many of the works I discuss here; a fellowship from the American Council of Learned Societies gave me the time to write and read; and being named a 2007 Carnegie Scholar gave me generous support for pursuing my ethnographic research in Egypt. The statements made and views expressed here are solely the responsibility of the author.

2. Talal Asad, "The Concept of Cultural Translation in British Social Anthropology" in *Writing Culture: The Poetics and Politics of Ethnography*, ed. James Clifford and George Marcus (Berkeley: University of California Press, 1986), 141–64.

3. This way of thinking about kinship is in line with what Michael Peletz describes as "the new kinship studies," though I read his review after I had developed my own argument. Especially helpful is his analysis of the theoretical paradigms that made new understandings of kinship as cultural and deeply imbricated in hierarchies of gender, race, and class, possible. I am especially sympathetic to his argument that studies of social practice reveal ambivalence at the heart of kin relations and that such ambivalence requires more analytical attention. See his "Ambivalence in Kinship since the 1940s" in Sarah Franklin and Susan McKinnon, eds., *Relative Values: Reconfiguring Kinship Study* (Durham: Duke University Press, 2001), 413–444.

4. Wendy Brown, *Regulating Aversion: Tolerance in the Age of Multiculturalism and Empire* (Princeton: Princeton University Press, 2006).

5. For a fuller description of this visit and the revelations about this incident that came when I returned nine months later, after the Haj passed away, see my essay, "A Kind of Kinship," in *Resident Aliens*, ed. Melvin Konner and Sarah Davis (Cambridge: Harvard University Press, in press, expected 2010).

6. For a broader discussion of how this community helps us think about women's rights, see Lila Abu-Lughod, "Preface for the Twenty-First Century," in *Writing Women's Worlds* (Berkeley: University of California Press, 2008), xi–xxiv.

7. For more on her pregnancy, see Lila Abu-Lughod, "A Tale of Two Pregnancies" in *Women Writing Culture*, ed. Ruth Behar and Deborah Gordon (Berkeley: University of California Press, 1995), 339–349.

8. Abu-Lughod, *Writing Women's Worlds*. Many are more familiar with this argument through my earlier article, "Writing Against Culture" in *Recapturing Anthropology: Working in the Present*, ed. Richard Fox (Santa Fe: School of American Research, 1991), 137.

9. United Nations General Assembly, 183rd Plenary Session in Paris on 10 December 1948, General Assembly resolution 217 A (III) *Universal Declaration of Human Rights* (UN Official Records: Geneva, 1948), 71–79. The text of the

Universal Declaration of Human Rights is available in 360 different languages on the website of the UN Office of the High Commissioner for Human Rights (http://www.ohchr.org/EN/Pages/WelcomePage.aspx). An English PDF of the resolution is available from that website at http://daccessdds.un.org/doc/RESOLUTION/GEN/NR0/043/88/IMG/NR004388.pdf?OpenElement.

10. Martha C. Nussbaum, *Women and Human Development* (New York: Cambridge University Press, 2000).

11. UN, *Universal Declaration of Human Rights*. The sentence quoted here is the first sentence of Article 1, 72.

12. Joseph Slaughter, *Human Rights, Inc.* (New York: Fordham University Press, 2007).

13. This historical specificity is not accepted by the historian, Lynn Hunt, whose history of human rights invokes the genealogy and links the development of human rights to sentiment produced by the novel. See Lynn Hunt, *Inventing Human Rights* (New York: W.W. Norton & Co., 2007).

14. Karen Engle explains why in an excellent article, "From Skepticism to Embrace: Human Rights and the American Anthropological Association from 1947–1999," *Human Rights Quarterly* 23, no.3 (2001): 536–559.

15. Gayatri Chakravorty Spivak, "Close Reading," special section on *The Humanities in Human Rights: Critique, Language, Politics. Publications of the Modern Language Association of America* 121, no. 5 (October 2006): 1608–1617, 1614. See also Lila Abu-Lughod. "Do Muslim Women Really Need Saving?" *American Anthropologist* 104, no. 3 (2002): 783–790 and "The Debate about Gender, Religion, and Rights: Thoughts of a Middle East Anthropologist," *Publications of the Modern Language Association of America* 121, no. 5 (October 2006): 1621–1630.

16. See the Convention's web pages, http://www2.ohchr.org/english/law/cedaw.htm, on the website of the UN Office of the High Commissioner for Human Rights, http://www.ohchr.org/EN/Pages/WelcomePage.aspx. The web pages include a short history of the Convention, as well as the text of it.

17. Sally Engle Merry, *Human Rights and Gender Violence* (Chicago: University of Chicago Press, 2006), 37.

18. Jane K. Cowan, Marie-Bénédicte Dembour, and Richard A. Wilson, *Culture and Rights: Anthropological Perspectives* (Cambridge: Cambridge University Press, 2001), 3.

19. Catherine MacKinnon, "Are Women Human?" in *Are Women Human?* (Cambridge: Harvard University Press, 2006), 41–43.

20. MacKinnon, *Are Women Human?* 43.

21. Charlotte Bunch, "Women's Rights as Human Rights: Toward a Re-Vision of Human Rights" *Human Rights Quarterly* 12, no. 2 (November 1990): 486–98.

22. Susan Moller Okin, *Is Multiculturalism Bad for Women?* (Princeton: Princeton University Press, 1999).

23. Bunch, "Women's Rights as Human Rights," 491.

24. Okin, *Is Multiculturalism Bad for Women?*, 10.

25. Brown, *Regulating Aversion*, 190.

26. Okin, *Is Multiculturalism Bad For Women?*, 23.

27. Brown, *Regulating Aversion*, 194.

28. Martha C. Nussbaum, "Non-relative Virtues: An Aristotelian Approach," in *The Quality of Life*, ed. Martha Nussbaum and Amartya Sen (Oxford: Oxford University Press, 1993), 265.

29. Martha C. Nussbaum, *Women and Human Development* (New York: Cambridge University Press, 2000), particularly "In Defense of Universal Values," 34–110.

30. Ibid., 97.

31. Ibid., 99 100.

32. For a discussion of these, see for example, Ridwan al-Sayyid, "The Question of Human Rights in Contemporary Islamic Thought" in *Human Rights in Arab Thought*, ed. Salma K. Jayyusi (London: I.B. Tauris, 2009), 253–73. For Iran, see Arzoo Osanloo, *The Politics of Women's Rights in Iran* (Princeton: Princeton University Press, 2009) and "The Measure of Mercy: Islamic Justice, Sovereign Power, and Human Rights in Iran" *Cultural Anthropology* 21, no. 4 (2006): 570–602.

33. Talal Asad, "Redeeming the 'Human' Through Human Rights," in *Formations of the Secular* (Stanford: Stanford University Press, 2003), 127–158.

34. Nussbaum, *Women and Human Development*, 78–9.

35. Asad, "Redeeming the Human," 150.

36. Martha C. Nussbaum, "Human Capabilities, Female Human Beings" in *Women, Culture, and Development: A Study of Human Capabilities*, ed. Martha C. Nussbaum and Jonathan Glover (Oxford: Oxford University Press, 1995), 85.

37. Ibid., 84.

38. Marilyn Strathern, "No Nature, No Culture: The Hagen Case," in *Nature, Culture, and Gender* ed. Carol P. Mac Cormack and Marilyn Strathern (New York: Cambridge University Press, 1980). See also Claude Lévi-Strauss, *The Savage Mind* (Chicago: University of Chicago Press, 1966); A.R. Radcliffe Brown, *Structure and Function in Primitive Society* (New York: The Free Press, 1965).

39. Nussbaum, "Human Capabilities, Female Human Beings," 63.

40. Dipesh Chakrabarty, *Provincializing Europe* (Princeton: Princeton University Press, 2000), 27.

41. Okin, *Is Multiculturalism Bad for Women?*, 16.

42. Leti Volpp, "Feminism versus Multiculturalism," *Columbia Law Review* 101, no. 5 (June 2001): 1204.

43. Ratna Kapur, "The Tragedy of Victimization Rhetoric: Resurrecting the 'Native' Subject in International/Post-colonial Feminist Legal Politics," *Harvard Human Rights Journal* 12 (2002): 1–37.

44. Volpp, "Feminism versus Multiculturalism," 1187; Uma Narayan, *Dislocations of Culture: Identities, Traditions, and Third World Feminism* (New York: Routledge, 1997). "Death by culture" is Narayan's phrase, quoted by Volpp.

45. Lila Abu-Lughod and Anupama Rao, "Gender, Human Rights, and the Global Locations of Liberalism," *Institute for Social and Economic Research and Policy (ISERP) Newsletter*, 3, no. 1 (Fall 2006), 6.

46. Nussbaum, *Women and Human Development*, 76.

47. This definition is attributed to the linguist Max Weinreich and was quoted in Chakrabarty, *Provincializing Europe*, 43.

48. Quotations from (in order) Gayatri Chakravorty Spivak "Can the Subaltern Speak," in *Marxism and the Interpretation of Culture*, ed. Cary Nelson and Lawrence Grossberg (Urbana: University of Illinois Press, 1988), 271–313 and Leila Ahmad, *Women and Gender in Islam* (New Haven: Yale University Press, 1992). The article has previously been cited: Lila Abu-Lughod, "Do Muslim Women Really Need Saving?" See also Charles Hirschkind and Saba Mahmood, "Feminism, the Taliban, and the Politics of Counter-Insurgency," *Anthropological Quarterly* 75, No. 2 (2002).

49. For a critique of *The Arab Human Development Report 2005* for its adoption of this language, see my "Dialects of Women's Empowerment: The International Circuitry of the Arab Human Development Report 2005," *International Journal of Middle East Studies* 41 (2009): 83–103. The original report was written in Arabic; for an English translation, see UN Development Programme, Regional Bureau for Arab States, *The Arab Human Development Report 2005: Towards the Rise of Women in the Arab World* (New York: United Nations Publications, 2006).

50. Chakrabarty, *Provincializing Europe*, 43.

51. Timothy Mitchell, "The Stage of Modernity" in *Questions of Modernity*, ed. Timothy Mitchell (Minneapolis: University of Minnesota, 2000), 3.

52. Chakrabarty, *Provincializing Europe*, 42.

53. See George Marcus and Michael Fischer, *Anthropology as Cultural Critique* (Chicago: University of Chicago Press, 1986) and Marshall Sahlins, *The Western Illusion of Human Nature* (Chicago: Prickly Paradigms Press, 2008), 106, 51.

54. Saba Mahmood, *Politics of Piety* (Princeton: Princeton University Press, 2005), 155.

55. Ibid., 199.

56. Paul Riesman. *Freedom in Fulani Social Life: An Introspective Ethnography*, trans. Martha Fuller (Chicago: University of Chicago Press, 1977).

57. Michael Jackson, *Existential Anthropology* (New York: Berghahn Books, 2005). These postcolonial and anthropological discourses have a kindred relation to some classics in feminist studies, like philosopher Maria Lugones' argument in "Playfulness, 'World'-Travelling and Loving Perception," *Hypatia* 2.2 (1987): 3–19, or Wendy Brown's brilliant new analysis of the civilizational thinking and intolerance that underlie and are reproduced by the increasingly popular contemporary liberal discourse of tolerance, *Regulating Aversion* (2006).

58. Arjun Appadurai. "Putting Hierarchy in its Place," *Cultural Anthropology* 3 (1988): 36–49.

59. Abdullah An-Na'im, *Human Rights in Cross-Cultural Perspective* (Philadelphia:

Temple University Press, 1992).

60. And to follow Asad, to ask who has the political power to redeem humanity (including human women) from "traditional cultures" or to reclaim for them their inalienable rights, which he says, "comes down in the end to the same thing." Asad, "Redeeming the Human," 154.

61. Merry, *Human Rights and Gender Violence*.

62. Chakrabarty, *Provincializing Europe*, 89.

63. I am referring here to the famous photography exhibit first shown at MOMA in 1952 that travelled the world. The curator had been, as O'Brian notes, "a member of a UNESCO committee established 'to study the problem of how the Visual Arts can contribute to the dissemination of information on the Universal Declaration of Human Rights.'" Meant to stress the "universal elements and aspects of human relations and experiences common to all mankind" the exhibit censored photographs of lynching and the effects of the atom bomb in Japan and was used as part of American propaganda in the Cold War setting. See John O'Brian's "The Nuclear Family of Man," *The Asia-Pacific Journal: Japan Focus* (July 11, 2008). I am arguing that family must be understood differently. http://www.japanfocus.org/_John_O_Brian-The_ Nuclear_Family_of_Man. Accessed February 24, 2009.

64. For an example of the range of this rethinking, see Sarah Franklin and Susan McKinnon, eds., *Relative Values: Reconfiguring Kinship Study* (Durham: Duke University Press, 2001).

65. For those familiar with my ethnography, *Writing Women's Worlds*, this is Kamla (a pseudonym).

66. I was pleased to find, after I had written this paper, that Marshall Sahlins, in his pamphlet, *The Western Illusion of Human Nature* (previously cited) noted on p. 44 that "the Western tradition has long harbored an alternative conception of order and being, of the kind anthropologists have often studied: kinship community. True that in the West this is the unmarked human condition, despite that (or perhaps because) family and kindred relations are sources of our deepest sentiments and attachments." He does not, however, consider the family as a complex mixture of power and attachment.

The Haunted World of Humanity: Ritual Theory from Early China

Michael Puett

I begin with a story about distant antiquity. The following is from the *Mencius*,[1] a text from the fourth century BCE that imagines an even earlier period in China, prior to the invention of agriculture:

> In the time of Yao, all under Heaven was not yet regulated. Flooding waters flowed throughout, inundating all under Heaven. The grasses and trees flourished, the birds and beasts multiplied, the five grains did not grow, the birds and beasts pressed in upon man, and the paths made by the hooves of beasts and the tracks of birds crossed throughout the central states. Yao alone was concerned about this.[2]

The text discusses Yao, a human in the midst of this chaos. Unlike other humans, Yao was concerned with what he saw around him, and he thus set out to change the world:

> He raised Shun to set forth regulations to deal with the situation. Shun put Yi in charge of fire. Yi set fire to the mountains and lowlands and burned them. The birds and beasts ran away and hid. Yu dredged the nine rivers, cleaned out the Ji and Ta and had them flow into the sea, cleared the Ru and Han and opened the Huai and Si and had them flow into the Jiang. Only then were the central states able to obtain food . . . . Hou Ji taught the people

to sow and reap the five grains. When the five grains ripened, the people were nourished. As for the way of the people, if they have full stomachs, warm clothes, and dwell in idleness without any education, they become close to animals. The sage was concerned about this and charged Xie to become the Supervisor of Education. He taught them using the relationships of man: fathers and sons have affection, rulers and ministers have propriety, husband and wife have differentiation, elder and younger have precedence, friends have trust.[3]

In short, order was created by humans domesticating the world and domesticating themselves. Prior to human domestication, humans and animals were not properly distinguished, wild grasses and forests flourished, and humans behaved like the birds and the beasts. Once humans burned the wilderness, domesticated the grains, and distinguished humanity from the (now-driven-away) animals, order emerged.

There are many such stories from early China. The *Xunzi*, a text from the third century BCE, makes a similar point in the form of a cosmological argument:

Therefore, Heaven and Earth gave birth to the superior man. The superior man gives patterns (*li*) to Heaven and Earth. The superior man forms a triad with Heaven and Earth, is the summation of the myriad things, and is the father and mother of the people. Without the superior man, Heaven and Earth have no pattern, ritual and righteousness have no unity; above there is no ruler or leader, below there is neither father nor son. This is called the utmost chaos. Ruler and minister, father and son, older and younger brother, husband and wife begin and then end, end and then begin. They share with Heaven and Earth the same pattern, and last for ten thousand generations. This is called the great foundation.[4]

According to this text, humans are born from Heaven and Earth. Heaven and Earth possess no pattern or order, and thus humans must create patterns in the form of a clear hierarchy to guide Heaven and Earth, as well as future humans. After these proper patterns are created, individual humans will come and go, but the proper patterns into which those humans will enter (ruler/minister, father/son, husband/wife) will endure as long as Heaven and Earth.

Although *Xunzi* does not develop it in this passage, the same argument could be made in terms of the narrative given in the *Mencius*: prior to human activity, the world of Heaven and Earth was chaos, with wild grasses and forests flourishing, with humans behaving as beasts, with water from the rains flowing across the lands. With human domestication, however, the world becomes properly patterned. Random rains from Heaven and wild grasses and forests from the Earth become ordered, such that the rains are now appropriated through irrigation to grow the grains that are now consumable by humans, and the humans thus nourished are now taught to live in proper relations with each other, instead of living like the animals.

In summary, both texts portray humans providing order to what was previously a chaotic natural world, transforming and domesticating that world so that it now functions as a patterned system: through human organization, Heaven and Earth now each play a crucial role, and the products of each are made meaningful and significant through human domestication. As *Xunzi* puts it, humans now form a triad with Heaven and Earth, with each performing a crucial function in an ordered cosmos: Heaven provides the seasons, Earth provides the raw foodstuffs, and humans provide the order that gives Heaven and Earth their proper place.

But, of course, the world does not always function this way: wild animals continue to infringe on human land, wild grasses continue to grow in agricultural fields, rains continue to be too plentiful and overflow the drainage systems, and humans continue to behave outside of the normative relationships that should guide their behavior. The attempt to place the world into a set of patterned relationships, in short, is a never-ending project. The domestication of the world is never complete.

Western Theories of Humanity

This may seem like an odd way to begin an essay on rethinking humanity. I do so because I would like to argue that these stories—or, rather, the philosophical impulse that underlies them and the ritual traditions that surround them—are of great interest in the larger project behind this volume. For well over a century, the dominant theories of humanity have been based upon traditions emerging in the Western world. Although more and more scholarship is being done on non-Western materials, such materials are almost always the object of our analysis: our theories are still almost entirely ones that arose recently in the West.

Over the past several decades, we have gone through a lengthy period of deconstructing these Western theories, showing the degree to which they are based upon Christian—often Protestant—narratives and assumptions.[5] But we have barely begun to undertake a rigorously anthropological study of humanity, in which we would not simply be studying many cultures but in fact learning from the indigenous theories of those cultures and taking them seriously as theory. An anthropology that is worthy of its name is one in which theories of humanity from, for example, China, South Asia, and Africa are taken every bit as seriously as those that emerged in the West.

In this essay, I would like to make a small step toward such a project by taking some of the indigenous theories concerning humanity that arose in early China and treating them as theory. "Theory" refers to general or abstract principles. As recent critiques of Western forms of knowledge have made clear, theories arise from historical specificities. In other words, while locatable, they are most often referred to in their abstracted or general form. What I am suggesting is a self-conscious creation of theory from a non-Western locale, where we consider some of the aspects of transforming a specific "local" or particular into a more generalized position. Needless to say, no theory is perfect—theories from China will not explain everything, nor will they be fully satisfying. Many will be infuriating. That is only to be expected. We take some ideas as theory to help us highlight aspects of the human condition. Of course, theories will also hide and obfuscate as well.

I would like to start by addressing a common objection to the sort of project I am advocating here. The argument of that objection might be as follows. Visions of humanity from early China are traditional: they are based in a traditional view of the world, and one that is now being replaced by a modern one. Such visions might be of historical interest to see how traditional societies thought about the world, and they might be of romantic interest for those who would like to reject the modern world, but they are hardly of wider interest to those who accept that, for better or for worse, we now do live in a modern world that has swept away or at least is in the process of sweeping away traditional societies and traditional modes of thought.

To respond to such an argument, and also to introduce some of the major assumptions that have defined much of contemporary theory, let us look in more detail at what is meant by the term "modernity." Put very broadly, much of what we call "modern" Western theory has been based upon assertions of discontinuity.[6] In terms of claims about modernity, the argument has been that, until very recently, all of humanity lived in so-called "traditional" cultures, meaning that humans would be born into a pre-given order that would define their position and place, along with a pre-given set of beliefs and a pre-given cosmology. According to this narrative, the modernity project then consisted of encouraging individuals to break from this traditional order and create a new world that allowed for autonomy, an assertion of free will, and the ability to control the universe around them. The ideal of such a world would be one of autonomous individuals living according to self-willed laws and making decisions based upon a rational calculation of benefit and cost. In the neo-liberal version of this narrative, the result would be a celebration of capitalism, which would be seen as wiping away such a traditional order and bringing to the fore an order of autonomous individuals engaging in economic activity in a rational free market.

Most economists would happily admit that such markets do not actually exist: they are ideals, by definition removed from the messy world.[7] The same is true of the other ideals mentioned: clearly humans do not really act as autonomous agents living according to self-willed laws and making decisions based upon a rational calculation of benefit and cost. The claim is we would be better off if we did, and hence the endless calls to assert autonomy.

In other words, the central move is to assert notions of autonomy over and against most of how we actually live our lives. This structure of argument pervades the reading of history. As we must endlessly assert our will over our mundane lives, so is the assertion of modernity as a whole a rejection of an earlier, traditional world. Of course we now begin to see modernity as a shifting target. There is always yet another "traditional" world from which to break. Yet the dominant theme characterizes "the modern world" as having made a decisive break from a "traditional" continuous world that somehow dominated all of humanity for thousands of years. The traditional/modern split includes within it a normative call for individuals to break from antiquated roles and closed cosmologies, to "gain agency."

Unfortunately, such readings of history have been so influential that what under this narrative would be categorized as "traditional" modes of thought are thus consistently read as having assumed a continuous, pre-given cosmology. Nowhere is this more so than so-called "traditional" China, frequently characterized as having assumed a harmonious, unified cosmos.

As should already be clear from the examples at the beginning of this paper, philosophical arguments from early China hardly assumed such a pre-given order.[8] Indeed, both of the texts argue explicitly that order can only be achieved through a dramatic human domestication of the given world. Immediately, it should be clear that our standard readings of this material from the perspective of a modernity paradigm are not fully accurate.

Many Western theories based upon claims of autonomy and modernity have come under fire recently. The past several decades have seen a flourishing of theoretical attempts to rethink the vision of an autonomous individual, usually in the form of trying to break it down, citing the danger of reifying the human as autonomous.[9] Such arguments, which would ultimately come under the label of "post-modernism," characterized attempts to define humans as autonomous agents as being themselves the primary problem. The solution thus entailed breaking down such claims to autonomy.

This critique of modernization theory often took the same structure as the object of the critique. If theories of modernity assumed a continuous order—say a traditional order—from which we must now break as autonomous individuals, many of the so-called "post-modern" theories have tried to critique this vision through a comparable move: there are autonomous individuals in our theoretical world and now we must break those individuals down yet further. If we can break down an "autonomous individual" and say the autonomous individual consists of multifarious things, that helps break down the dangers of falling into visions of individualism, autonomy, will, etc. In other words, for this approach, more discontinuity continues to be the goal.

The Fractured World of Humanity

I would like to introduce a body of theory from early China that poses the problem for humanity and therefore the solutions for humanity in a different way. These theories are of particular interest because they pose the problem of fractured experience as being very much the opposite of how many contemporary theorists see the problem of the fragmented subject.

These theories are abstracted from the texts I introduced above that hinted at how, in early China, the fundamentally fractured and fragmented nature of human experience in the world was posited as the primary problem. If we take these particular texts to the level of theoretical generality, the theory of the human would read as follows:

We live in a world in which things in what we call the cosmos happen at irregular times. At times, it rains, it gets cold, it gets hot—sometimes there seems to be a pattern to all of this, but oftentimes the changes do not follow such a pattern. Moreover, even what we call the individual is a conglomeration of energies, emotions, and desires, many of which can be quite dangerous and can lead people to do horrible things to each other— even to those within their immediate families.

That comes to an end when people die. But then they become ghosts who haunt the next generation, with the energies of anger and jealousy being directed at those still alive. The living are thus constantly haunted by ghosts. Everything we have done in the past and everything previous generations have done will haunt us until we die. Our energies then do the same to the next generations.

The world we face, in other words, is always fragmented and fractured, and the fundamental problem for humans therefore is not to fragment it further or assert more discontinuity. The problem for humans is to begin the process—and it will never end—of trying to create connections and build a more ethical world from the fragmented one of our experience.

But only for brief periods is this likely to succeed. I emphasize brief because the theories I am talking about are inherently tragic in their ultimate implications. The human transformation of the world can never fully succeed. In our mundane lives, we try to build pockets of order for brief periods of time before they inevitably fall apart.

The body of theory I will be discussing takes this as its central problem: if what humans face is a fragmented and fractured world, then how do we build these pockets of order in which for brief periods of time we are good to each other, we help each other, we inspire others to be better, we bring out our better energies and inspire others to do the same—until, inevitably, negative energies flourish again and we try to build a new order yet again. We live in a world of endless sets of relationships—of our energies within us, of ourselves with others and with things in the world—and many of these relationships are negative. Like animals, we are drawn by our immediate desires, until we are consumed by other animals drawn by the same insatiable energies. This body of theory sees the problem as one of improving those relationships by refining our responses, controlling what come to be seen as our lesser desires, and transforming ourselves and the larger world such that better relationships can flourish.

If the results will inevitably be tragic, the efforts are nonetheless crucial. For only humans can create a better world. As *Xunzi* put it in the quotations given above, "only humans can give pattern to the world." In these theories, then, the solution was not to assert discontinuity—either by asserting autonomy or by breaking down a claim of autonomy by asserting yet more discontinuity. Discontinuity and fragmentation were rather the problems that needed to be solved.

This has been abstract.[10] This next section will discuss more concretely how these theories solve what they perceive as a fundamental problem in the human condition.

Refining One's Dispositions

A theory from the text known as "Nature Emerges from the Decree" goes along the following lines.[11] We humans exist in a world in which there are things—the Chinese term used here (*wu*) refers to any thing, including humans. These things each have their natures. The world then consists of these things as they interact with each other in every situation—endlessly coming into contact with each other, drawing out reactions from each other. With humans, our natures include various energies—what we would call our emotional dispositions. The various situations we are in pull out these energies—a given situation will make us happy, sad, angry, and so on:

> The energies of joy, anger, sorrow, and sadness are given
> by nature. When it comes to their being manifested on
> the outside, it is because things (*wu*) have called them
> forth.[12]

Often, the resulting interactions will be harmful for other human beings and the rest of the world. This text also claims that humans alone have the possibility of forging a better form of interaction, instead of simply having their energies drawn out by whatever situation they encounter:

> As for the Way's four techniques, only the human way
> can be way-ed [i.e., only the human way involves a fixed
> purpose]. As for the other three techniques, one is
> moved and that is all.[13]

According to the text, we should not try to get rid of these energies since they are an inherent part of humans. Instead we seek moments in our lives retrospectively—or, as the tradition builds up, in past historical periods—when for whatever reason humans have related well to each other. It could have simply been by accident. That makes no difference. All that matters is that, at a certain moment, a good response occurred. The goal is then to take that moment and make it into a ritual—which means having people re-do it, developing that same dispositional sense that occurred at that moment when (surprisingly) people acted well toward each other, thus inculcating in themselves the proper energies associated with that good response. Over time, a tradition of ritual repertoires accumulates from which humans slowly learn different ways of guiding their emotions, and thus slowly learn to have better dispositional responses toward those around them. These repertoires of ritual also train the next generation to have better dispositional responses toward those around them.

Through ritual, humans learn as they grow up that using a certain bodily motion or tone of voice affects other human beings in a certain way. When we meet someone what tone of voice do we use? What bodily language? Out of these commonplace and mundane issues, more profound issues start to be addressed. How can we live our lives in such a way that affects others for the better? How can we ultimately work to build a society in ways that work for the better?

As the text says, "The rites arise from the dispositions . . ."[14] The rituals are what came to be regarded later as good dispositional responses, which are then made into rituals to help refine the dispositional responses of those who come later. As with the domestication of the world through agriculture, the rituals are not a purely artificial construction: they depend on taking phenomena in the world and working with them and transforming them—in this case, transforming the dispositional responses into a normative set of actions.

Ghosts

And then we die. But when we die, the next generation has to live with what we have done—perhaps literally living with our ghosts.

Thus far we have been talking about ways of improving our own dispositional responses to those around us. But among those things everyone has to deal with is the past. We are haunted all the time by what came before. Thus, just as we must build up rituals for dealing with things around us, we must do the same with the dead.

What are the dispositional ways we can guide our emotions to act well with such ghosts? In a literal sense this will involve changing the ghosts into ancestors. Or, if the ghost is not one of the things we can consider as part of our lineal kin, then transforming that ghost into a god. Either way, our goal is to develop a relationship to that past in a way that we hope will transform us through our ritual actions toward it, transform everyone else who sees this process going on, and perhaps influence that past energy and transform it as well.

The "Meaning of Sacrifices" chapter from *The Book of Rites* discusses this transformation.[15] As is often the case in early China, the initial creations of these rituals are ascribed to sages—humans who were able to see how to work with phenomena to create a better world. In this text, the description of the creation of the rituals is put in the mouth of another sage, Confucius:

> Zai Wo said: "I have heard the names 'ghosts' and 'spirits,' but I do not know what they mean."
> The Master [i.e., Confucius] said: "The energies (*qi*) are the flourishing of spirit; the earthly souls (*po*) are the flourishing of the ghost. Combining the ghost and the spirit is the highest teaching."[16]

The text continues with Confucius speaking:

> Everything that is born will die. When one dies, one returns to the ground. This one calls the "ghost." The bones and flesh wither below; hidden, they become the earth of the fields. Their energies (*qi*) are sent out above; they become radiant brightness. According with the essence of things, instituting the pivot of action, [the sages] clearly named "ghosts" and "spirits," taking them as a pattern for the black-haired people.[17]

Or to put it more simply: when someone dies, some of those energies float up into the heavens, while the earthly souls (*po*)—along with the flesh and the bones—return to the ground. As human beings we need to create a ritual way of relating to these two sets of things. Confucius continues his explanation:

> The sages took this as still insufficient, so they constructed dwellings and houses, and set up temples and ancestral halls. They thereby differentiated closer and more distant kinship, and closer and further removed in terms of descent. [The sages] taught the people to turn to the past and look back to the beginning, no longer forgetting where they came from.[18]

After creating places for the different kinds of remains of the dead, the sages then created rituals for the living to perform to each:

> When these two ends were established, they [the sages] responded with two rituals. They set up the morning service, burning fat and manifesting it with the radiance of [burning] southernwood. They thereby responded to the energies (*qi*). This taught the populace to return to the beginning. They offered millet and rice, and served liver, lungs, head, and heart, presenting them and separating them into two bowls, and supplementing them with sacrificial wine. They thereby responded to the earthly souls (*po*). This taught the people to love one another, and taught superiors and inferiors to utilize their dispositions. This was the utmost of ritual.[19]

Thus, the "spirits," the energies that float into the heavens, would be worshipped as ancestors—ranked into a lineage and then worshipped according to lineage rank in an ancestral hall. This forces the living to create relationships with them in their role as figures in a lineal relationship to those still alive. Doing so constantly reinforces the sense among the living of the degree to which we are based on what came before, the degree to which we should be beholden to what came before. The energies that remain on the ground—the earthly souls, flesh, and bones—would be placed in a tomb. A feast would be the ritual, performed in order to promote proper familial feelings toward the immediately deceased kin.

For example, if one's father were to pass away, one would worship his energies as an ancestral spirit in the sense of one's lineage relationship to it: he would be an ancestor one generation above, and would in turn be the descendant of ancestors above him. In contrast, what one would worship at the tomb would be the father as a family member, to whom one would strive to have proper familial feelings.

In both cases, of course, the relationships built with the ancestral spirit and the tomb occupant are very different from the relationships with that person while alive—relationships that would often have been fraught with difficulties, negative energies, and so on. But we are now striving to develop proper, ritual relationships with these two remains of the person, normative relationships that will by definition be distinctive from the complex relationships we really had with that person while alive. The ritual energies we are now worshipping, and the proper relationships we strive to develop toward them, are based upon the normative ritual visions of how we ought to relate to our family members. By performing these ritual relationships, those alive hope to have a better relationship with the next generation. The inherent disconnect between the proper relationships we are striving to develop toward the ancestral spirit and the tomb ghost, and the relationships we actually had with that person while alive, is part of what makes the rituals efficacious.

We try to bring ghosts, spirits, and the past that haunts us into a ritual order in which we are transformed by developing better relationships with them—proper ritual relationships that will then, if we perform them well, improve the way we relate not only to the past but also to those currently living among us.

A Ritual World of Perfection

In understanding the implications of these arguments, I would like to underline how different these theories are from those that might typically be attributed to a "traditional" worldview. These theories do not argue for a passive acceptance of a pre-given order, nor do they assume a continuous, harmonious cosmos. On the contrary, they emphasize the brokenness of the world. These theories call for humans to transform themselves and the world ceaselessly in order to create better relationships. Indeed, as the texts at the beginning of this paper argue, the domestication of the world is an absolute necessity, and something only humans can do.

The goal is thus neither to accept a pre-given, continuous order nor, as in a modernity narrative, break from such a continuous order and assert individual autonomy. The goal as discussed above is to work ceaselessly to transform the world—to create a continuous, harmonious order, even though this is by definition impossible for anything more than brief periods of time.

The practice uses repeated actions to create a ritual world composed of perfect relationships—the equivalent of the domesticated world of human agriculture described in the first quotations from *Mencius* and from *Xunzi*, which also saw human domestication of the natural world in agriculture as related to the domestication of humans in the world of ritual. In this ritual world of normative relationships, humans would behave well toward each other and would maintain a perfect relationship with the past.

But, of course, the world does not really operate this way. Just as, in the agricultural sphere, wild grasses grow in our fields, the rains do not come when we need them, and people starve because the natural processes do not fit into the patterns we require for our domestication, so do human emotions spill beyond the ritual patterns we create, and so do humans continue to behave horribly toward each other.

As Arthur Kleinman has written so eloquently, things are stubborn—they resist our interpretations, our narratives, our attempts to construe the world as we would hope.[20] By creating a ritual world in which people act properly toward each other, and by having people perform these proper ritual relationships on a recurrent basis, the hope is that we can continually train ourselves to have better dispositional responses in the nonritual world of fragmentation and discontinuity.

As some colleagues and I have argued elsewhere,[21] ritual thus creates a subjunctive world of "as if," which operates and in part gains its power from the disjunct ritual creates with the world of our own experience: if we experience a world of fragmentation and discontinuity, haunted by ghosts and capricious spirits, then we create a ritual world of flawless continuity, in which everything is perfectly related to everything else. The training of our dispositions in the perfect relationships of ritual helps us to deal with the flawed and often vicious relationships outside ritual.

In the example of ancestral worship, we worship the deceased in its ideal state—as a perfect ancestor above, and as a perfect family member in the tomb. Of course, the person while alive was not perfect, nor were we perfect toward that person while alive. The inevitable disjunct between that ideal and the actual complexities of the person and our relationships with that person while alive is one of the reasons the rituals can be so effective: that disjunct becomes part of what the practitioners experience, and this allows them to inculcate within themselves an ideal to which they can strive, perhaps doing better than the generations before.

The Tragic World of the Ghosts

Thus, by performing these rituals, we hope to create better dispositional responses to those around us and to what came before, slowly building up a better world. If we do this, then for brief moments of time we can create such a better world, a more ethical world for those around us in which we may inspire those around us to be better human beings and in which we can deal with the past effectively and productively.

By definition the process can never end. We are always constructing better relationships to others, to our past, and to history. Inevitably our attempts fail. Humans still have negative energies, and will still behave horribly to each other. New situations will emerge. We will have to develop yet more relationships based upon them and try to work with those as well. These attempts to transform the world can never succeed fully.

With rituals of ancestor worship, it is an endless attempt to—at a literal level—place elements of the past into specific places where we can then deal with them effectively. Ultimately this always fails: the ancestors are never fully ancestors, they are also ghosts who continue to haunt us. Despite our best efforts, the ghosts are still there. They will never fully become ancestors, nor will we ever fully relate to them as ancestors. When the past comes back as ghosts, either literally or figuratively, as a past that haunts us, we have to deal with that as well.

Or putting this in an historical sense, it means that the past is always there. Events accumulate, and our attempts to build narratives to deal with these events and relate well to them will inevitably be insufficient. So, as we develop these narratives and ways of relating to the past that inevitably fail, and these—speaking literally or metaphorically—ghosts continue to haunt us, we then strive endlessly to build up new ways of relating to the past, and new ways—again literally or figuratively—of placing the ghosts into places where we can deal with them. And this too will inevitably fail, thus producing the need for yet more responses.

It is a vision that says from day one we face a broken world haunted by ghosts, and what we as humans do is endlessly cultivate our emotions with other human beings through a ritual repertoire, endlessly trying to construct a better world yet knowing that we will never succeed for any length of time. At most, what we will get are brief pockets of order.

This emphasizes the need for humans to strive continuously to build and re-build the world. Underlying the surface pessimism is an optimistic vision of what humans are capable of doing. If this is what we can aim for, if this is all we can aim for, then it ought to be the entire focus of human life: in our daily lives being as good toward other human beings as we can, endlessly developing this ritual repertoire to improve ourselves and those around us. We can become, for brief pockets of time, better human beings, affecting those around us for the better: a seemingly tragic vision, but also a powerful and optimistic one.

This view does not assume that humans should be striving for autonomy or will. We should accept the inevitability of a world in which we are constrained by what came before, constrained by negative energies we have within us, constrained by the stubbornness of things which by definition will resist our attempts at control and domestication. Given this stubbornness of things, the goal is to endlessly develop ways of refining and transforming our relationships with them and those around us such that we gradually become better human beings.

This vision brings to the table a fascinating way of thinking about becoming better human beings not through abstract notions of autonomy or will, not through visions of how we break from something that came before—breaking from a traditional order, or declaring our autonomy from things that constrain us—but rather accepting a world in which we are inherently constrained and then working, I will again use Arthur Kleinman's terminology here, to give care to those around us.[22] Spending a life slowly building a somewhat better order, knowing that we will fail but knowing in the attempt to do so we will help others and perhaps leave a legacy that will enable others who come after us to build upon it further. A powerful way of thinking about the human condition and an inspiring vision of what it means to be a human living our common, mundane, everyday lives in ways that we hope will, for brief periods of time, affect those around us for the better.

NOTES

1. *Editor's note:* all translations by author. [Bracketed items are author's interpolations.]
2. *Mencius* or *Mengzi*, 3A/4 (Hong Kong: Chinese University of Hong Kong, Institute of Chinese Studies, Ancient Chinese Text Concordance Series [hereafter referred to as ICS], 1995).
3. Ibid.
4. *Xunzi*, "*Wangzhi*" (Hong Kong: ICS, 1996), 9/39/3–6.
5. Marshall Sahlins, "The Sadness of Sweetness: The Native Anthropology of Western Cosmology," *Current Anthropology* (1996) 37.3; Talal Asad, *Genealogies of Religion: Discipline and Reasons of Power in Christianity and Islam* (Baltimore: Johns Hopkins University Press, 1993).
6. For an excellent discussion of theories of modernity, see Jürgen Habermas, *The Philosophical Discourse of Modernity*, translated by Fredrick Lawrence (Cambridge: MIT Press, 1991).
7. See, for example, Milton Friedman, *Essays in Positive Economics* (Chicago: University of Chicago Press, 1953).
8. There are, of course, texts from early China (such as the *Baihu tong*) that try to argue that the cosmos is a unified, harmonious order upon which humans should model themselves—a position with which the texts I discuss in this paper would have strongly disagreed.
9. See, for example, Jacques Derrida, "The Ends of Man," in *Margins of Philosophy*, translated by Alan Bass (Chicago: University of Chicago Press, 1982), 109–136.
10. It has also been very ahistorical. For those readers who would like more background on the creation of these ritual texts and the impact they later had on Chinese history, see Michael Puett, "Human and Divine Kingship in Early China: Comparative Reflections," *Religion and Power: Divine Kingship in the Ancient World and Beyond*, edited by Nicole Brisch (Chicago: Oriental Institute of the University of Chicago, 2008), 199-212. In this paper, however, I will intentionally pull these arguments from their historical context and instead treat them as theory—not just applicable to aspects of early Chinese practice but also of potential interest to us today. Indeed, it is important to point out that, even when they were written, these were arguments about what one should do, not descriptions of actual practice. Not only can they be read as applicable to more than just early China, they are not even necessarily the best guides for understanding early Chinese ritual practice.
11. The text in question is the *Xing zi ming chu*, ("Nature Emerges from the Decree"), excavated from the Guodian tomb. For fuller discussions of the text, see Sarah Allan and Crispin Williams, editors, *The Guodian Laozi: Proceedings of the International Conference, Dartmouth College, May 1998* (Berkeley: The Society for the Study of Early China and Institute of East Asian Studies, University of California, 2000); Ding Sixin, *Guodian Chumu zhujian sixiang yanjiu* (Beijing: Dongfang chuban she, 2000); Guo Yi, *Guodian zhujian yu*

xian Qin xueshu sixiang (Shanghai: Shanghai jiaoyu chuban she, 2001); Michael Puett, "The Ethics of Responding Properly: The Notion of *Qing* in Early Chinese Thought," in *Love and Emotions in Traditional Chinese Literature*, edited by Halvor Eifring (Leiden: Brill, 2004), 37–68; Michael Puett, "Innovation as Ritualization: The Fractured Cosmology of Early China," *Cardozo Law Review* 28:1 (October 2006), 28–30.

12. *Xing zi ming chu*, strips 2–3, *Guodian chumu zhujian*, 179.
13. Ibid., strips 14–15, 179.
14. Ibid., strips 16–18, 179.
15. The text in question is the "Meaning of Sacrifices" chapter (*Ji Yi*) of the *Book of Rites (Liji)*. The *Book of Rites* would ultimately become one of the Five Classics, part of the standard educational curriculum for the educated elite throughout much of East Asia, and would accordingly become one of the most significant bodies of ritual theory throughout East Asia. See *Liji* (Hong Kong: ICS, 1992), 123–129.
16. Ibid., 126/25/24.
17. Ibid., 126/25/25–27.
18. Ibid., 126/25/28.
19. Ibid., 126/25/29.
20. See Kleinman's paper at the beginning of this book and also Arthur Kleinman, *Writing at the Margin: Discourse Between Anthropology and Medicine* (Berkeley: University of California Press, 1997) and *The Illness Narratives: Suffering, Healing, and The Human Condition* (Boston: Beacon, 1988).
21. Adam Seligman, Robert Weller, Michael Puett, and Bennett Simon, *Ritual and its Consequences: An Essay on the Limits of Sincerity* (Oxford: Oxford University Press, 2008).
22. See Arthur Kleinman's *What Really Matters: Living a Moral Life amidst Uncertainty and Danger* (Oxford: Oxford University Press, 2007).

Notes on Contributors

Volume Editors

J. Michelle Molina (PhD, University of Chicago, 2004) is John W. Croghan Assistant Professor in Catholic Studies at Northwestern University. In 2007-08, she was a research associate with Harvard Divinity School's Women Studies in Religion Program. She is currently working on a book manuscript tentatively titled "The Jesuit Ethic and the Spirit of Global Expansion." The book examines the method and purpose of the Ignatian Spiritual Exercises—a meditative retreat geared toward self-reform, their relationship with early modern global expansion, the role of women's spiritual activism in popularizing the Exercises among the laity and the impact that this Jesuit program of radical self-reflexivity had on the formation of colonial selves. Prior to HDS, she served as Assistant Professor of Transregional Religion at the University of California-Irvine. Her fields of interest include transregional religious history, Jesuits, gender and subjectivity, early modern Europe, and colonial Latin America.

Donald K. Swearer is Distinguished Visiting Professor of Buddhist Studies at Harvard Divinity School (HDS) and serves as Director of the Center for the Study of World Religions. Before coming to HDS in 2004, Professor Swearer taught at Swarthmore College since 1970, most recently as the Charles and Harriet Cox McDowell Professor of Religion. His main research areas are: Theravada Buddhism in Southeast Asia, primarily in Thailand, and Buddhist Social Ethics. His current research interests focus on sacred mountain traditions in northern Thailand as well as Christian identity in Buddhist Thailand. His recent books include *Ecology and the Environment* (2009, which he edited); *The Buddhist World of Southeast Asia* second revised edition (2009); *The Legend of Queen Cama: Bodhiramsi's Camadevivamsa, a Translation and Commentary*

(1998), *Sacred Mountains of Northern Thailand and Their Legends* (2004), and *Becoming the Buddha: The Ritual of Image Consecration in Thailand* (2004). Professor Swearer has held a variety of editorial posts for several academic journals, including the *Journal of Asian Studies,* the *Journal of Religious Ethics,* and *Religious Studies Review,* and taught several courses on religion and ethics.

Contributors

Lila Abu-Lughod, the Joseph L. Buttenwieser Professor of Social Science at Columbia University, has focused on three broad issues in her strongly ethnographic, mostly Egypt-based work: the relationship between cultural forms and power; the politics of knowledge and representation; and the dynamics of gender and the question of women's rights in the Middle East. Her most recent ethnography, *Dramas of Nationhood: The Politics of Television in Egypt* (2005), a contribution to the anthropology of nations and to media ethnography, explored the tensions between the social inequalities besetting nations and the cultural forms that aspire to address them. In a number of edited books, she has pursued these themes further to examine questions of gender and modernity in postcolonial theory, of anthropology and global media, and of violence and national/cultural memory. Currently, as part of an effort to use anthropology to contribute to larger political debates, she is focusing on the universalist claims of liberalism and on the ethical and political dilemmas entailed in the international circulation of discourses of human rights in general, and Muslim women's rights in particular.

Veena Das is Krieger-Eisenhower Professor in the Department of Anthropology at Johns Hopkins University; previously she taught at the University of Delhi and at the New School University in New York City. Her research interests include feminist movements, gender studies, sectarian violence, medical anthropology, post-Colonial and post-Structural theory, South Asia, and Europe. The unifying theme of her research has been developing understanding of the institutional and cultural logic embedded in contemporary events, particularly in violence and suffering. Among her many publications are most recently *Life and Words: Violence and the Descent into the Ordinary* (2007), *Structure and Cognition* (second edition, 1996), and several influential edited volumes. Currently she is working on a project on disease and health-seeking behavior among the urban poor in Delhi in collaboration with the Institute of Socio-Economic Research in Development and Democracy to track the relationship between local ecology, health, and family processes of decision making.

Charles Hallisey, Senior Lecturer on Buddhist Literatures at HDS, joined the HDS faculty in 2007 after teaching at the University of Wisconsin as Associate Professor in the Department of Languages and Cultures of Asia and the Religious Studies Program since 2001. Earlier, he taught in the Department of Theology at Loyola University in Chicago, and at Harvard University, where he was John L. Loeb Associate Professor of the Humanities in the Committee on the Study of Religion and the Department of Sanskrit and Indian Studies from 1996 to 2001. His research centers on Theravada Buddhism in Sri Lanka and Southeast Asia, Pali language and literature, Buddhist ethics, and literature in Buddhist culture. He is currently working on a book project entitled "Flowers on the Tree of Poetry: The Moral Economy of Literature in Buddhist Sri Lanka."

Arthur Kleinman, M.D., is one of the world's leading medical anthropologists, and a major figure in cultural psychiatry, global health, and social medicine. He is the Esther and Sidney Rabb Professor, Department of Anthropology, Harvard University; Professor of Medical Anthropology in Social Medicine and Professor of Psychiatry, Harvard Medical School; and Victor and William Fung Director of Harvard University's Asia Center. Since 1968, Kleinman, who is both a psychiatrist and an anthropologist, has conducted research in Chinese society, first in Taiwan, and since 1978 in China, on depression, somatization, epilepsy, schizophrenia and suicide, and other forms of violence. His chief publications are *Patients and Healers in the Context of Culture* (1980); *Social Origins of Distress and Disease: Depression, Neurasthenia, and Pain in Modern China* (1986); *The Illness Narratives* (1988); *Rethinking Psychiatry* (1988); and the co-edited volumes: *Culture and Depression* (1985) and *Social Suffering* (1997). His most recent book, *What Really Matters* (2006), addresses existential dangers and uncertainties that make moral experience, religion, and ethics so crucial to individuals and society today.

Michael Puett is Professor of Chinese History in the Department of East Asian Languages and Civilizations at Harvard University. He received his PhD in 1994 from the Department of Anthropology at the University of Chicago. His interests are focused primarily on the inter-relations between religion, anthropology, history, and philosophy. He is the author of *The Ambivalence of Creation: Debates Concerning Innovation and Artifice in Early China* (2001) and *To Become a God: Cosmology, Sacrifice, and Self-Divinization in Early China* (2002), as well as the co-author, with Adam Seligman, Robert Weller, and Bennett Simon, of *Ritual and its Consequences: An Essay on the Limits of Sincerity* (2008).

Index